Simple, Clear, and Correct
Sentences

William J. Kelly
Bristol Community College

PEARSON

Boston   Columbus   Indianapolis   New York   San Francisco
Upper Saddle River   Amsterdam   Cape Town   Dubai   London   Madrid
Milan   Munich   Paris   Montréal   Toronto   Delhi   Mexico City
São Paulo   Sydney   Hong Kong   Seoul   Singapore   Taipei   Tokyo

Senior Acquisitions Editor: Matthew Wright
Senior Supplements Editor: Donna Campion
Marketing Manager: Thomas DeMarco
Production Manager: Ellen MacElree
Project Coordination, Text Design, and Electronic Page Makeup:
 Integra
Cover Designer/Manager: John Callahan
Cover Image: Getty Images
Senior Manufacturing Buyer: Roy L. Pickering, Jr.
Printer and Binder: R. R. Donnelley/Harrisonburg
Cover Printer: R. R. Donnelley/Harrisonburg

Library of Congress Cataloging-in-Publication Data
Kelly, William J. (William Jude), 1953–
    Simple, clear, and correct: sentences/William J. Kelly.
    p. cm. — (The simple, clear, and correct series)
Includes index.
ISBN 13: 978-0-205-52086-2
ISBN 10: 0-205-52086-3
    1. English language—Rhetoric   2. English language—Sentences.
3. English language—Grammar.   I. Title.   II. Series.
PE1408.K4758 2012
808′.042—dc22

                                                                2011007384

1 2 3 4 5 6 7 8 9 10—DOH—14 13 12 11

ISBN-13: 978-0-205-52086-2
ISBN-10: 0-205-52086-3

Dedication

To my daughter Jacqueline—
Being your father is a constant—and enormous—
source of personal joy and pride.

The *Simple, Clear, and Correct* Series

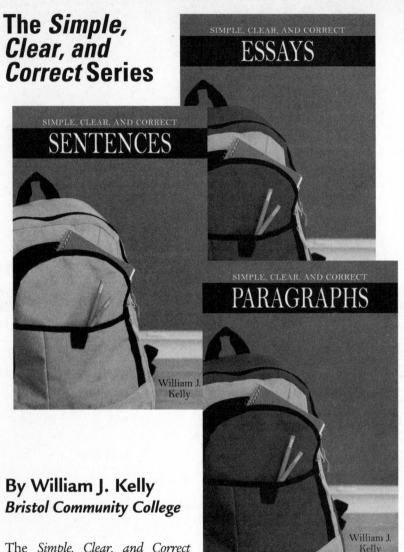

By William J. Kelly
Bristol Community College

The *Simple, Clear, and Correct* series includes three brief, very affordable books: one on *Sentences*, one on *Paragraphs*, and one on *Essays*. The presentation and features of the *Simple, Clear, and Correct* series ensure that the subject matter in all three books is appealing and easy to comprehend. The language is accessible and uncomplicated, and specific, relevant examples illustrate each principle. Meaningful writing activities, including plentiful topics for exploration, appear throughout each book. All three books feature an effective use of white space and gray-screen effects, plus a carefully designed system of headings to serve as a clear guide through the material. Presented in an easy-to-handle 6 by 9 trim size and a total of 272 pages, all three books follow the advice of the title: *simple, clear*, and *correct*.

Contents

CHAPTER 7 Example 61

Overview: Offering an Illustration 61
A Clear Direction with Multiple Supporting Illustrations and Details 62
Specific Supporting Illustrations and Details 62
Relevant Supporting Illustrations and Details 63
Effective Arrangement and Sufficient Transition 63
An Example Checklist 64
An Annotated Example Writing 64

CHAPTER 8 Process 67

Overview: Outlining the Steps 67
A Clear Focus and Simple, Logical Steps 68
Appropriate Use of the Imperative Mood 68
Reasonable Expectations and Necessary Cautions 69
Linear Order and Sufficient Transition 69
A Process Checklist 70
An Annotated Process Writing 71

CHAPTER 9 Definition 74

Overview: Specifying Meaning 74
A Clear Direction and the Elements of an Effective Definition 75
Approaches to Develop an Extended Definition 75
Appropriate Personal Interpretations or Experiences 76
Effective Arrangement and Sufficient Transition 77
A Definition Checklist 78
An Annotated Definition Writing 78

CHAPTER 10 Comparison and Contrast 81

Overview: Examining Similarities and Differences 81
Specific Subjects and Focus 82
A Clear Basis of Comparison and Contrast 82
A Thorough and Specific Presentation 83
An Effective Arrangement and Sufficient Transition 83
A Comparison and Contrast Checklist 85
An Annotated Comparison and Contrast Writing 86

CHAPTER 11 Cause and Effect 89

Overview: Understanding Reasons and Ramifications 89
A Clear Direction and Appropriate Focus 90
Direct and Related Causes and Effects 90

Preface

Consider all the different documents you have read in your life. Now think of your favorite piece, the one that stands out from the rest. It doesn't matter if it is a book, a print or online article, a blog, a personal essay, a set of instructions, a long e-mail from a friend, or something else. What makes you judge it as good and effective?

The answer is probably more complicated than you might realize. A successful piece of writing is the sum of many things, and the truth is that no formula, no set of blueprints, exists that always results in a document that works. But what you are also likely to find is that good writing is consistently *simple, clear,* and *correct*—it is focused and direct, easy to follow, and free from errors. However, good writing can never fulfill its promise if it isn't in correct sentence form, which is why *Simple, Clear, and Correct: Sentences* consistently emphasizes the importance of writing well at the most basic level: the sentence.

To foster greater understanding and mastery of writing, *Simple, Clear, and Correct: Sentences* provides a thorough introduction to the stages of the writing process as well as discussions of the rhetorical modes, with plenty of illustrations and examples. The result is a complete tour through what a writer must do in order to develop and express effective *content* on a subject. At the same time, the book also offers extensive coverage of key elements of the significant problems with grammar and usage, including sentence fragments, comma splices, run-on sentences, subject–verb agreement, modifier and pronoun use, and spelling. This attention to matters of *form* helps ensure that the good ideas developed during the writing process will be expressed in a structure that communicates their full meaning: the complete sentence. As the title of the book indicates, all this information—the material on content and the material on form—appears in simple, clear, and correct terms.

Arrangement of the Text

Simple, Clear, and Correct: Sentences is divided into four sections. Part I, "The Writing Process—From First Thoughts to Final Draft," includes four chapters. The first chapter, "Effective Writing: Process and Product," dispels some self-defeating myths associated with writing and offers an overview of the stages of the writing process. It also discusses the relationship between writer and reader and introduces two familiar writing applications, the paragraph and the essay, stressing that the common denominator in these documents is the sentence.

The next three chapters—Chapter 2, "The Prewriting Stage"; Chapter 3, "The Composing Stage"; and Chapter 4, "The Revising Stage"—carefully examine the writing process. Each chapter features specific, concrete examples and explanations, including annotated models, exercises, and activities for immediate practice, all with a simple, basic goal: the creation of a paragraph of 100–150 words that has a main point, supporting examples, and a closing sentence. Together, these chapters clearly illustrate how a journey through the writing process results in a piece of writing that is simple, clear, and correct.

Part II, "The Modes: The Organizational Strategies and Approaches," features nine chapters that introduce the rhetorical modes: *narration, description, example, process, definition, comparison and contrast, cause and effect, division and classification,* and *argument.* Each mode is discussed as an organizing technique or pattern that is used to help communicate a clear meaning to a reader. Argument, however, is discussed as an aim or *purpose* rather than a type.

Each chapter in Part II contains a thorough explanation of the characteristics of that particular mode along with a practical checklist. Each chapter also includes a brief annotated writing that illustrates the principles presented and serves as a model for good writing. Each chapter further includes topics for writing that are both interesting and accessible, making it easy to put the principles into practice in the form of a 100- to 150-word paragraph.

Chapter 13, "Argument," illustrates how to present and support a stance on a controversial subject. It stresses the value of including supporting information from experts and the importance of properly acknowledging that information. In addition, the chapter includes a valuable list of common logical fallacies, with clear examples and specific solutions.

Part III, "Issues of Mechanics and Usage," consists of four chapters covering the foundation of grammar and usage, including the parts of speech (Chapter 14), the parts of a sentence (Chapter 15), the types of sentences (Chapter 16), and the classifications of sentences (Chapter 17). These chapters review the information that all writers must understand in order to express their ideas in simple, clear, and correct sentences.

Part IV, "Common Problem Spots—Identification and Elimination," includes ten chapters focusing on finding and correcting the kinds of errors that so often lead to faulty sentences. These weaknesses include the three significant errors in sentence structure: fragments (Chapter 18) and comma splices and run-on sentences (Chapter 19). Also covered are strategies for avoiding errors within sentences, including subject–verb agreement (Chapter 20); regular and irregular verbs, as well as verb tense and voice (Chapter 21); nouns and pronouns (Chapter 22); adjectives, adverbs, and other modifiers (Chapter 23); spelling (Chapter 24); parallelism (Chapter 25); punctuation (Chapter 26); and capitalization and numbers (Chapter 27). Effective writing is a marriage of solid content and correct form. With this nearly even split between information on generating and expressing ideas and information on expressing those ideas in acceptable standard English, *Simple, Clear, and Correct: Sentences* provides exactly what writers need to succeed.

Features of the Text

The design and presentation of *Simple, Clear, and Correct: Sentences* maximize its effectiveness and ease of use. Key features include:

- simple and highly accessible language throughout
- clear, easy-to-understand examples that illustrate all aspects of the writing process
- numerous engaging and relevant opportunities for writing
- a focus on brief writings—100-150 words—with emphasis on a main point, supporting ideas, and a closing sentence
- annotated examples of all stages of the writing process and of the modes
- practical checklists to evaluate progress in all aspects of writing
- simple, clear explanations of errors in form, making identification and elimination of mistakes easy

- a carefully designed system of headings that serves as a clear guide through the text
- an attractive page layout, featuring an effective use of white space and gray screen effects
- an easy-to-handle 6 by 9 trim size

In short, *Simple, Clear, and Correct: Sentences* fulfills the promise of its title. It accentuates the importance of the basic unit of writing—the sentence—and does so simply, clearly, and correctly.

Acknowledgments

I wish to offer thanks to a number of people for the help and support they provided while I was working on *Simple, Clear, and Correct: Sentences*. First of all, I remain deeply grateful to John M. Lannon, University of Massachusetts, Dartmouth (retired), and Robert A. Schwegler, University of Rhode Island. Their guidance and their wisdom—and their friendship—mean more than they could ever know. I also want to acknowledge the long-standing encouragement of Paul Arakelian, University of Rhode Island; Paul F. Fletcher, Professor Emeritus, Bristol Community College; and Jack R. Warner, Executive Director of the South Dakota Board of Regents for Higher Education.

I owe thanks to a number of my colleagues at Bristol Community, including Catherine Adamowicz, Gabriela Adler, Debbie Anderson, Denise DiMarzio, Elizabeth Kemper French, Michael Geary, Tom Grady, Jeanne Grandchamp, Farah Habib, Deborah Lawton, Arthur Lothrop, Diane Manson, Diana McGee, Linda Mulready, Jean Paul Nadeau, Joanne Preston, and Howard Tinberg.

The following instructors from across the country kindly provided suggestions that shaped the text, and I thank them for sharing their expertise and insight: Shawn Adamson, Genesee Community College; Janna Anderson, Fullerton College; Elsie Burnett, Cedar Valley College; Cathy Fagan, Nassau Community College; Debra Farve, Mount San Antonio College; Ellen Gilmour, Genesee Community College; Ruth Hatcher, Washtenaw Community College; Sandra Hooven, University of Las Vegas; Noel Kinnamon, Mars Hill College; Kathy Parrish, Southwestern College; Rebekah Rios-Harris, Cedar Valley College; Cynthia VanSickle, McHenry County College; and William L. Young, University of South Alabama. Thanks also to Nicole C. Matos, College of DuPage, and Timothy Matos, Truman College, for their assessments and recommendations. That Nicole and Tim also happen to be my older daughter and son-in-law is truly my good fortune.

In addition, I owe thanks to a number of people on the Pearson team who worked so hard on my behalf. First on that list is Matthew Wright, Senior Acquisitions Editor, Basic English and Developmental Writing, who from the start of this project has demonstrated nothing but unwavering support. Also deserving my thanks are Samantha Neary, Editorial Assistant; Sue Nodine, Project Editor for Integra–Chicago; and Ellen MacElree, Project Manager for Pearson, for guiding the book through production and publication and for making the final product look so good.

Finally, I want to offer thanks to my family. My late parents, Mary R. and Edward F. Kelly, taught my brothers and me lessons about life and learning that continue to resonate. I am also grateful to my parents-in-law, Flo and Leo Nadeau, and my sons-in-law, Jeremy Wright and Timothy Matos; and I am prouder than anyone could ever know to be the father of Jacqueline M. Wright and Nicole C. Matos—and the grandfather of Alexander Owen Matos.

Most deserving of my thanks, however, is my wife, Michelle Nadeau Kelly. For nearly forty years now, I have been the beneficiary of her intellect, her humor, and her kindness. I am profoundly grateful for her confidence in and support for my teaching and my writing and, far more important, for her love, more than words can convey.

WILLIAM J. KELLY

PART I

The Writing Process: From First Thoughts to Final Draft

Effective Writing: Process and Product

The Components of Effective Writing

For many people, few things are more frustrating—or more intimidating—than facing a writing task. If you are one of those people, you've probably done whatever you could, both in school and outside the classroom, to avoid writing.

Maybe you've even told yourself that being able to write is not that important, that you can do a better job *saying* your ideas than writing them down. Maybe you've told yourself that nobody would be able to understand what you write anyway because you are a terrible speller and you can never keep the rules of grammar and usage straight. Worst of all, maybe you've told yourself that you have nothing to say that anyone else would care about, so why bother learning how to write?

But here's the thing—these beliefs aren't true. Being able to express yourself through speech is, of course, important, but being able to write your ideas simply, clearly, and correctly is even more important for you, both in college and on the job. The rules of English grammar, usage, and spelling can be confusing, but their difficulty isn't greater than your ability to master them. And make no mistake about it: you have worthwhile things to say, things that other people will find interesting.

The secret is not to let that sense of intimidation and frustration take over. Mastering writing takes time, patience, and practice—plenty of practice. The more you write, the more confident you'll become, and you'll soon find that confidence leads to competence.

The Writing Process

Writing isn't a random act. It is not simply a matter of sitting down, thinking of ideas, and having those ideas flow down from your brain through your arm and out onto a computer screen or piece of paper. Rather, it's a *process*—a series of stages—that will help you meet the needs of your reader as you express your ideas in *complete sentences* that make up a *paragraph* or an *essay*.

The first stage, *prewriting*, involves generating ideas on a subject and identifying a specific focus or direction for writing. Many informal prewriting activities exist, including reading, taking part in a discussion, viewing a movie, observing behavior, and so on. Chapter 2 introduces a number of more structured prewriting activities proven to help you uncover and discover ideas for writing.

The second stage, *composing*, entails adapting or elaborating on the ideas you developed during prewriting so that their meaning is clear and then expressing them in complete sentence form. During this stage, you explicitly state your main point—the focus of the piece of writing—and expand and explain your prewriting ideas so that they offer the clearest, most specific support for that main idea, a step called *amplifying*. The version that results is called the *first draft*.

The third stage of the process, *revising*, consists of carefully evaluating the first draft and making any necessary changes and adjustments in terms of unity, coherence, and language. With revising, the goal is to build on what is already effective in the piece of writing while also eliminating errors and clarifying weak or confusing material. Once you thoroughly *edit* and *proofread*, the first draft becomes an *effective final draft*.

Keep in mind that the writing process is *recursive*, which means that you move back and forth through the stages as often as necessary. The following visual illustrates how the process works:

1

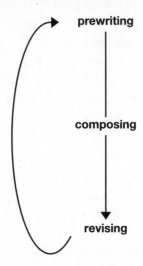

First you prewrite, and then, as the arrow in the center of the illustration shows, you move to composing and then to revising.

But notice that the arrow flows from revising back to prewriting. That's because once you identify any gaps and weaknesses in the piece of writing, you need to head back to prewriting to generate additional information to address those problems. Then you go back through composing and revising, during which you amplify and edit. The result of this process is an effective final draft that is simple, clear, and correct.

MASTERY EXERCISE 1 Considering Writing Problems and the Writing Process

1. Which do you find easier to do, explaining your ideas aloud or writing them down? Why do you think this means of communication is easier for you?
2. Besides in your previous English or writing classes, name one experience or circumstance in or out of school for which you had to complete some writing. What did you find difficult about this writing situation?
3. Take another look at the discussion and visual about the writing process (pages 3–4), and think of the last time you had to complete a piece of writing. On which stage of the writing process did you spend the most time? On which stage did you spend the least?

The Writer–Reader Relationship

When you write, you are not alone in the process, or, rather, you shouldn't be. In almost all cases, what you write is for someone else: your reader. How you handle your relationship with your reader will determine the ultimate effectiveness of what you write.

The following visual illustrates this relationship:

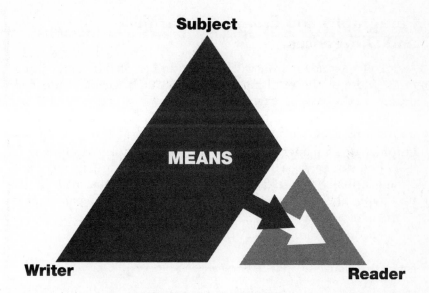

As this diagram shows, when you write, you as the writer communicate your point about your subject to your reader, using written language as your means.

The darker portion of the triangle, on the left, represents your ideas on the subject. Notice the space between this section and the smaller portion to the right. A gap always exists between you and your reader. That's because you have a specific level of understanding and insight about your subject that your reader doesn't necessarily have.

To fill this gap, you have to anticipate your reader's questions about your subject and develop examples and details that will answer those questions and make your point about the subject clear. In other words, you need to explain what you mean fully, in terms that someone other than you can easily understand. When you do so, you maintain a solid relationship with your reader.

Sometimes you will know exactly who your reader is, for example, when you write an e-mail message to your supervisor at work or a note to a friend who has experienced a personal loss. However, for

1

much of the writing you'll do, your reader won't be clearly identified, so you may find it easier to focus on the *average reader*.

Think of yourself *before* you learned detailed information about your subject. What kinds and degree of information did you need to know? The average reader is just like you were then and, in order to make sense of what you are writing about, needs the same type and number of examples and details that you needed in order to understand the subject.

Paragraphs and Essays: Similarities and Differences

As a college student, you will face a number of different writing tasks. Most of the resulting documents can be divided into two groups on the basis of length and scope.

Sometimes you will be asked to write a fairly limited series of unified sentences that support a main point, a unit known as a **paragraph.** When a paragraph stands alone as a complete document, it will often run between 150 and 250 words. It will usually include a closing sentence that restates or reemphasizes the point made in the paragraph. The following figure shows the structure of a paragraph:

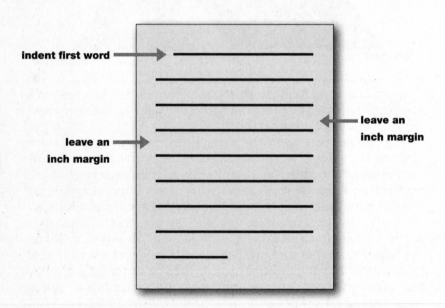

As the figure illustrates, you indent the first line about a half-inch, with each subsequent line following it and flowing from the left to the right margins.

Other times you'll be asked to prepare a far more detailed document in which several paragraphs work together to support or illustrate your main point. Such a multiparagraph document is called an **essay.** The following figure shows an essay's structure:

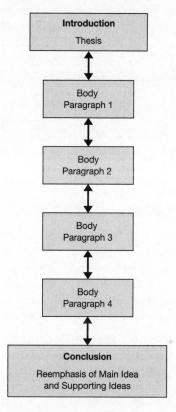

The introductory paragraph indicates the subject and direction of the essay, sparking the reader's interest. The body paragraphs support and illustrate the main point expressed in the introduction. The minimum number of paragraphs constituting the body is three, but essay paragraphs are usually shorter than stand-alone paragraphs. An essay often runs between 500 and 750 words, so a body containing ten or more of these shorter paragraphs isn't unusual. The concluding paragraph brings the essay to a logical and appropriate end, often reiterating or summing up the main idea.

For all their differences in scope, length, and structure, paragraphs and essays have one thing in common: They must be written in sentences. Your success as a writer therefore depends in large part on your learning to write simple, clear, and correct sentences, which is what the material in this book will help you do.

1

MASTERY EXERCISE 2 **Considering the Connections between Writer and Reader and between a Main Point and Supporting Information**

1. A gap always exists between you and your reader in terms of specific knowledge of your subject. What should you do to fill that gap so that your reader can more easily understand what you are saying?
2. How can thinking in terms of the average reader help you be sure to supply details and examples to make your subject clear and understandable?
3. Make a copy of a passage of about 300–400 words from a newspaper, magazine, or Internet article or from one of your other textbooks. For each paragraph in the passage, highlight, circle, or underline the main point. Then choose one of the paragraphs and explain how the rest of the sentences support the main point.

Summary Exercise

1. Consider the discussion that opens this chapter about the frustration and intimidation that many people report when faced with a writing task. What has been the most difficult writing situation you have faced in school or beyond the classroom? What was it about that experience that made it so hard for you? What was the outcome of the experience?

2. Your goal as a writer is to create documents that stand out because they make a point effectively. In your life thus far, you have read many, many documents—short stories, poems, articles, novels, and so on. Of all those texts, which one is your favorite? In your view, what does the writer of this piece do that makes it so memorable for you?

3. As page 3 briefly explains, prewriting, during which you develop a focus and supporting ideas and details, is the first stage of the writing process. A handful of informal prewriting techniques— reading, taking part in a discussion, viewing a movie, observing behavior—are named. Choose one of these activities and briefly explain how taking part in this activity could help you develop ideas for writing.

4. Think of a current or former job. Imagine that you were going to leave that job and have to train your replacement. What are the three most important things that you would tell a newcomer about this position to bridge the gap of information between the two of you? Why would you share these three points?

2

The Prewriting Stage

Techniques for Prewriting

The first step of successful writing is planning. As the last chapter indicated, prewriting is the stage in the writing process during which you do this planning. It involves generating material on some topic and developing a specific focus. The information produced will enable you to develop a piece of writing that is simple, clear, and correct.

Basically, any method you use to develop initial ideas on a subject is acceptable. For instance, if you like to go off by yourself and think, grab a cup of coffee and talk about your subject with friends or classmates, flip through books or newspapers, or consult online sources to see if you can find any useful information, you're doing fine because you're planning.

In addition to these kinds of activities, a number of more structured prewriting techniques are available to you. Among the most common are **freewriting, brainstorming, clustering,** and **branching.** Each method allows for a slightly different approach to this vital part of the writing process. Your goal at this point is to try each technique in order to discover which method—or which combination of methods—best suits your own style of work.

2

Freewriting and Brainstorming

When it comes to prewriting, two techniques that have proven to be effective are *freewriting* and *brainstorming*. Both strategies involve listing words and phrases that come to mind in relation to a topic. They differ in terms of scope and the time involved.

Freewriting involves a set period of time, usually around ten minutes, during which you take a subject and, without making any conscious effort to control your ideas or present them in correct form, write down or type whatever words come into your head. If your mind goes blank or you feel silly, simply write, "I can't think" or "I feel stupid" until something else comes to mind. Don't worry if you repeat yourself or make mistakes. The only way to freewrite incorrectly is to stop writing. The goal of freewriting is to generate as much material as you can. Sorting through the material comes later, as with all prewriting techniques.

Consider this freewriting on *childhood*:

Childhood, let's see—don't remember much, guess memories start when I began school. Mrs. Greves—that was her name, liked her, pretty much the first teacher I can remember. Wonder where she is now? TV shows and movies about childhood—not usually accurate. Am I getting off track a little? No worries when I was a kid, not many, at least, no responsibilities—not like now. Kids have it made. Still not easy for a lot of them now, violence in schools, not time to just go out and play. My allowance, bought candy and the only work to do was sweep up and make my bed, OK, what now? can't write anything—can't think anything!! Stuck! All right, how about this—was I happy then? Little things made me happy, like staying up late to watch TV or winning at cards with my sister. Do kids today even play cards?

Right now, of course, the ideas are in rough form, but a number of them hold promise. That's frequently how it works with freewriting. When you let the ideas flow without stopping them or editing them in any way, potential areas of development that might not have made it to the page or screen often appear. As this example illustrates, you should highlight, underline, or circle your best prewriting ideas. Then you'll be prepared to develop these ideas more fully as you continue to work through the rest of the writing process.

Brainstorming is similar to freewriting in that you begin with a general subject and don't concentrate on errors in form. With brainstorming, however, you more deliberately focus on the subject and write or type only the ideas that are directly related. In addition, you don't set as deliberate or restricted a time limit as you do with freewriting. With brainstorming, you will probably generate fewer ideas than with freewriting, but you will also probably end up with a group of ideas that have more obvious connections.

Take a look at the following brainstorming on *exercise:*

Reasons to make sure to exercise

- People-lots of them-are way overweight, obese really
- Working out-weight training, kick-boxing, yoga, all ways to stay in shape
- More energy-drag through the day when I don't exercise
- Less stress
- Ran two miles after that argument-I needed that
- Good health guaranteed, some doctors say

Reasons some people don't exercise

- Too busy-after work, school, family stuff
- Not great progress at first-can be discouraging
- Embarrassing to be with people in better shape

2

Like the freewriting, this brainstorming contains a number of possibilities for development, but the list is somewhat more limited than the freewriting because you've been more deliberate and selective in terms of what you've written down. The good news is that the ideas are likely to be directly related, and, in some cases, can serve as a rough, informal outline for further development.

MASTERY EXERCISE 1 Practice with Freewriting and Brainstorming

1. Choose two of the following subjects. Using the models in the previous pages to guide you, complete a freewriting for the first and a brainstorming for the second.
   - luck
   - relaxation
   - a surprising experience from the workplace
   - my last birthday
   - fame
2. Identify the most promising ideas in both your freewriting and your brainstorming and highlight, circle, or underline them.
3. Choose one of these ideas and list three additional examples, details, or illustrations that you might use to develop and support this idea.

Clustering and Branching

Freewriting and brainstorming are fairly conventional in that they involve a format that we associate with writing: words and phrases recorded on a page either in lines or in a listing of some kind. Two additional proven prewriting techniques—*clustering* and *branching*—are less conventional in that they involve recording ideas in a more visual, graphic form.

With clustering, you let your ideas spread out in multiple directions instead of across a page or in a column, with lines indicating the specific connections. To begin, you write a general topic in the middle of a page and circle it. As related ideas pop into your head, write them down on the page around the topic, circle each of them, and draw lines to connect these related ideas to the topic. As your initial ideas lead to new ones, write them down and circle them as well, connecting them with lines. This sample clustering, on *money*, shows what happens when you follow this process:

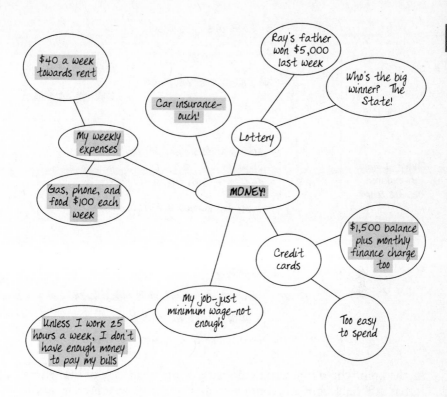

As this example shows, clustering enables you to explore a subject from multiple directions and perspectives. The lines illustrate the connections between ideas and help to identify the most promising ones.

Branching also emphasizes the connections between ideas. Working left to right across a page, you explore your subject while emphasizing the connections between the information you generate. First, you list your subject on the left edge of a piece of paper, roughly in the center. Write the items that your topic inspires to the right of the first point, linking the ideas with lines. Then allow these new ideas spark new points, and so on, letting the information spread across the page, as the following example on *personal duties or responsibilities* shows:

2

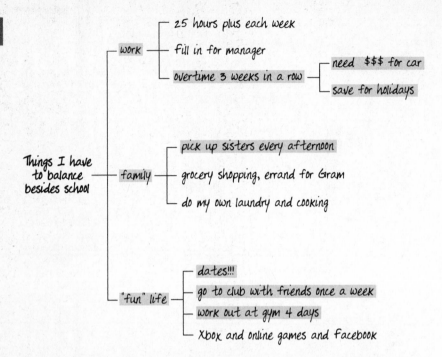

As the highlighted material demonstrates, an advantage of branching is that different segments contain related examples, so it is often easier to organize information later in the writing process.

MASTERY EXERCISE 2 Practice with Clustering and Branching

1. Choose two of the following subjects. Using the models in the previous pages to guide you, complete a clustering for the first and a branching for the second:
   - advertisements
   - an important relationship
   - a vivid memory from school
   - music
   - hopes for the immediate future
2. Identify the most promising ideas in both your clustering and your branching and highlight, circle, or underline them.
3. Choose one of these ideas and list three additional examples, details, or illustrations that you might use to develop and support this idea.

The Best Prewriting Technique—or Combination of Techniques—for You

2

Effective writing begins with prewriting. The exploration and planning involved in this key step create the foundation you need to succeed. Therefore, you need to identify which technique matches the way you most prefer to work. You might even decide that a combination of techniques—a *hybrid* prewriting strategy—is the best choice for you. Always use the approach that best enables you to focus on a topic and generate supporting ideas, examples, and illustrations.

Summary Exercise

1. Now that you have tried the different prewriting techniques, identify which approach you prefer and briefly explain why you feel it matches the way you prefer to work.

2. Using the technique you prefer, prewrite on one of the following topics:

   • a time you were caught in a lie
   • an important personal quality
   • a dream vacation
   • the best place to live
   • the one thing people need to be happy

3. Highlight, circle, or underline the most promising ideas and identify a focus—a main idea.

4. Using the material you have developed, create a writing of about 100–150 words that communicates your ideas so that someone else—your reader—will understand them as you do.

3

The Composing Stage

From Basic Ideas to First Draft

Once you have developed preliminary information through prewriting, you move to the second stage of the writing process, **composing.** In this stage, you specify the direction you want to take—your **main point**—and convert the most promising ideas into **supporting sentences.** During the composing stage, you must turn your attention to matters of **form**—grammar, usage, spelling, punctuation, and so on. Your goal is to create an effective **first draft,** one that expresses your good ideas simply, clearly, and correctly.

A Clear Main Point

To make sure that you supply a specific direction for your reader, you need to provide a clear main point. When the document you prepare is a paragraph, this main point is known as a **topic sentence,** and when the document is an essay, it is known as a **thesis.** In either case, the main idea is like a neon sign signaling the reader what will be discussed.

The sentence expressing the main idea generally consists of two parts: your subject and *your attitude about* or *reaction to* that subject. Consider this example about children and pets:

16

subject

Clear Main Point: *Pets, even simple ones like goldfish or hamsters,*

attitude or opinion

should never be given to very young or immature children.

This main idea is clear because it informs the reader of both the subject and the attitude or opinion about that subject.

To be sure that your main point is clear, make sure that it is NOT

- a simple announcement, featuring expressions like *I plan, I intend,* or *This writing will discuss:*

Ineffective: I want to explain that parents shouldn't give pets to very young or immature children.

- a statement of fact, leaving no room for discussion or debate:

Ineffective: Owning a pet is popular in the United States.

- a title, which is intended to provide only a broad hint of the subject and is not usually a sentence:

Ineffective: When to Give a Child a Pet

MASTERY EXERCISE 1 Distinguishing between Effective and Ineffective Main Points

1. Consider the following list of sentences. If the sentence could serve as an effective main point, label it **E** in the space provided. If it is ineffective because it is an announcement, a statement of fact, or a title, label it **I**.

    _____ a. YouTube is so much fun.

    _____ b. Society will never experience serious progress until people stop believing in religious, gender, and racial stereotypes.

    _____ c. Today, many people work, stay in touch with their friends, and play computer games in small restaurants and coffee shops with free Wi-Fi connections.

    _____ d. Lots of Americans are in bad shape.

    _____ e. Crisis in Education

3

_____ f. The federal government needs to begin an aggressive bridge inspection program to keep a terrible tragedy from occurring.

_____ g. This writing will discuss the movement by some businesses to use Twitter and other social networking sites to advertise and stay in touch with clients and customers.

_____ h. Fulfilling the American Dream

_____ i. The frantic search at a beach for a missing child was a truly upsetting experience.

_____ j. I want to talk about how brutal and bloody an ultimate fighting match can be.

2. Choose one of the sentences that you have identified as ineffective. First, explain why it could not serve as a good main point in its present form, and then rewrite it so that it is effective.

The Development of a Main Point and Selection of Supporting Examples and Details

Sometimes you will know the main point of your writing right from the moment you begin prewriting. In a writing class, for example, you might choose or be asked to write on a subject about which you are already interested and have knowledge. As a result, you will already know how you want to address the subject, which makes developing your main point easier.

Other times, however, your focus will appear or take shape as you identify the most interesting ideas generated during prewriting. It's likely that one or more examples or details will stand out or be connected or related to each other in some way. Other ideas will probably explain or illustrate these points further, which in combination will suggest or inspire a direction for you to pursue.

If you decided to write on some aspect of the subject of _confidence_ and used freewriting to explore it, you might end up with something like this:

Confidence? Lots of people have it, people you see in sports or in business or even dancing. I wish I had more self-confidence-always feel that I can't

3

do things, like sports, just shake with worry before games and track meets, sure I am going to make a mistake-I hate the pressure-have trouble with tests, too, especially essay tests-the worst, sociology, couldn't answer two questions -and I knew the answers. Just freeze up, maybe test anxiety? Always sick the night before even quizzes. Actors, musicians, people like that must have a lot of confidence, teachers must have it too-have to talk in front of people all the time-can't think-when I had to give that 3-minute speech in American history last year, felt like an hour, like that time shooting foul shots in middle school during the championship. And dating, the worst! I'm afraid people won't like me-always sick before I go out, and a huge headache after even if things went OK. Jeremy and Jacqueline-they are so confident.

The highlighted ideas indicate the effects that a lack of self-confidence has had, so the next step is to express these ideas in a draft version of your clear main point, which can be adjusted later on to make it more exact:

Main Point: My lack of self-confidence keeps me from being as successful as I could be.

With your main point expressed clearly, you can look through your prewriting material and identify the ideas that provide the best support.

The highlighted material concerns three general areas affected by a lack of self-confidence: sports, dating, and school. If you were creating a longer document like an essay, you would be able to discuss all three categories. But for a single paragraph of 100–150 words, you should concentrate on the category for which the strongest and most complete support exists.

3

The material about sports and dating is good, but it is a bit limited at this point. But the examples and details related to school-work, shown here, are stronger and more complete:

- have trouble with tests, too, especially essay tests
- the worst, sociology, couldn't answer two questions—and I knew the answers
- just freeze up, maybe test anxiety?
- Always sick the night before even quizzes.
- when I had to give that 3-minute speech in American history last year, felt like an hour

It makes sense, then, to make this information the focus of your writing.

MASTERY EXERCISE 2 Developing a Draft Main Point and Supporting Information

1. So far, you have completed prewritings on a number of subjects. Choose the one that you like best or one that you feel holds the most potential for development. Or, if you'd prefer, prewrite on one of the following subjects:
   - life in a big city or small town
   - driving adventures
   - integrity

   Using the sample freewriting above to guide you, carefully evaluate the prewriting to identify a focus and then develop a draft main point.
2. From the prewriting, choose at least five details or examples that would offer solid support for your main point. If you need additional details, prewrite again to generate new information, this time on the specific subject addressed in your draft main point.

The Difference between Writer-Centered Ideas and Reader-Centered Material

3

Right now, most, if not all, of your prewriting ideas are **writer centered** because they are incomplete. These examples, illustrations, and details make sense to you as the writer because you have a more thorough understanding of them than the words on the page indicate. But for your ideas to communicate your meaning, they need to be **reader centered.** They must appear more completely and in a simple, clear, and correct form that makes sense to someone else: your reader.

To make your writing reader centered, think of yourself before you learned about your subject. What kinds of specific examples and details helped you understand? Your reader will need the same kinds and number of examples as you needed.

In general, you can expect your reader to know a little bit about many subjects but to lack the specific knowledge about the subject you are discussing, especially if it concerns a personal experience or is complex or unusual in any way. The following **Reader Evaluation Checklist** will help you make sure the information you include as support is reader centered.

To use the Reader Evaluation Checklist below, simply insert your topic in the blank spaces, and then write your answers to the questions.

READER EVALUATION CHECKLIST

❏ What does my reader need to know about _____?

❏ What does my reader probably already know about _____?

❏ What information would help my reader better understand _____?

❏ What did I find the hardest to understand about _____ at first?

❏ What helped me to figure out _____?

❏ What's the best example or explanation I can give my reader about _____?

The answers to these questions will help you adjust and improve the information you have already developed as well as create any additional supporting examples and details needed to communicate your full meaning to your reader.

3

Effective Supporting Details and Examples: Amplifying

To transform writer-centered examples and details into reader-centered examples and details, you need to express them in full, specific detail and in correct sentence form. In other words, you need to **amplify** them.

Consider this writer-centered detail from the prewriting on the effects of a lack of self-confidence:

Writer Centered: sociology, couldn't answer two questions—and I knew the answers

Expressed this way, this information fails to communicate its full meaning to your reader. It isn't clear, complete, or correct.

Now consider the same information after it has been amplified:

Reader Centered: On my sociology exam last week, I couldn't complete two of the brief essay questions even though I knew the answers. I was just too nervous.

This reader-centered version is clearly better. It has been amplified with additional clarifying information. Just as important, the material is now expressed in correct sentence form. As a result, it is far easier for your reader to understand the point being made.

MASTERY EXERCISE 3 **Identifying Solid Supporting Ideas and Transforming Writer-Centered Information into Reader-Centered Material through Amplifying**

1. The following sentences are too general and limited to communicate a full meaning. They are therefore writer centered. Choose three of them and then rewrite them with enough specific information that another reader will be able to understand what the sentence is actually discussing.
   a. I really enjoy that show because it is entertaining.
   b. Overall the experience was confusing.
   c. To get better, you need to be devoted.
   d. That one innovation has led to so much change.
   e. Most people have never even visited one.

3

2. For Mastery Exercise 2 (page 20), you developed a draft main point and generated five details or examples that could be used as support. Now, make these supporting ideas reader centered by amplifying them, using the above discussion about amplifying to guide you.

An Effective Method of Arrangement and an Appropriate Closing

Once you have identified and developed the supporting ideas, you should consider the most effective way to arrange them so that they help you fully support your main idea. You will often find that you turn to one of three common methods of arrangement:

- chronological order—arrangement on the basis of time
- spatial order—arrangement on the basis of physical location relative to other things
- emphatic order—arrangement on the basis of importance or significance

If you were writing about an embarrassing incident that you experienced or an accident you witnessed, chronological order would enable you to recount the series of incidents involved. If you were discussing the layout of a campground or amusement park you visited as a child, spatial order would help you describe it. If you were asserting that public schools should run year-round or that superstars who have used steroids should be not be allowed to be named to the Hall of Fame, emphatic order would enable you to build your case from strong reason, to stronger reason, to strongest reason.

Some of the examples in the list of details and examples on self-confidence and school are stronger than others, so emphatic order would be a good choice, as this informal outline shows:

A Bad Effect: becoming sick before assignments are due
A Worse Effect: dealing with anxiety while giving a speech
The Worst Effect: being too tense to answer questions on an essay test even though you knew the answers

To bring a piece of writing to a complete and appropriate end, you should also include a closing of some type. With a longer document like an essay, this closing would be a brief paragraph called a **conclusion.** But with a writing of about 100–150 words, you would conclude your ideas by adding a **closing sentence.**

In general, the closing sentence should restate in some way the point expressed in the main point and supporting ideas. With the writing about a lack of self-confidence, you might create a sentence like this:

Closing Sentence: I wish I knew a magic formula for self-confidence because I am sure my life would be better.

This sentence restates the desire for and importance of self-confidence, so it is an effective closing sentence.

MASTERY EXERCISE 4 Considering the Proper Order of Arrangement and Appropriate Closing

1. For the previous two Mastery Exercises, you created a draft main point and supporting information that you transformed into reader-centered examples and details. Now, after reviewing the discussion of possible methods of arrangement (page 23), decide what order will best communicate your meaning to your reader and prepare an informal outline. Use the example on page 23 to guide you.
2. Consider the significance of your draft main point and the supporting points. Then, using the closing sentence on the need for greater self-confidence (page 24) as a model, create a closing sentence that will effectively conclude your writing.

A Rough Draft and a First Draft

At this point, you've taken a number of steps to turn your prewriting ideas into a successful piece of writing. You have developed a main point, identified promising supporting ideas, and created additional ideas if necessary. You have also amplified these examples and details and considered the best way to arrange them. Now you are ready to create a complete version or **draft** of your writing. This document won't be perfect, but it will be a complete piece of writing, which is what you need for the next stage in the writing process: **revision.**

You should actually create two initial versions, a **rough draft** and a first draft. The rough draft is for your eyes only. After you complete your rough draft, take a brief break, maybe an hour or so, to clear your head. Then reread what you have written, eliminating any obvious errors in form or problems with clarity. The version that results is your **first draft.** This is the draft that you can share with others for their reactions and suggestions as you move to revision.

Prepare your rough and first drafts on a computer. Take full advantage of the computerized grammar and spell check features. While not foolproof, they will help you find and eliminate many errors in grammar, usage, and spelling. Be sure to double-space.

In most cases, your instructors will expect your final versions of written documents to be prepared in this format anyway. An added advantage of double-spacing at this stage is that during revision, you can print out a copy of your first draft and have the room you need to make corrections and add new material by hand. Then you can return to the original word-processing file, make the changes, and print out your final draft for submission.

So now you have your main point, amplified supporting points and a plan for arranging them, and a closing sentence. What happens when you put them all together? Here is the first draft discussing the effects that a lack of self-confidence can have on a college student:

The **main point** identifies the focus of the writing. Note how the addition of the phrase *especially in school* to the draft main point specifies the specific direction.

The **examples** and **details** from the prewriting have been **amplified** and *offer support for the main point.*

My lack of self-confidence is keeping me from being as successful as I could be, *especially in school*. Most of the time, I am physically sick the night before assignments are due. Then there is the anxiety. I had to give a three-minute speech in American history last year, and it was bad. Have trouble with tests, too, especially essay tests. On my sociology exam last week, I couldn't complete two of the brief essay questions even though I knew the answers. I was just too nervous. **I wish I knew a magic formula for self-confidence because I am sure my life would be better.**

The **closing sentence** restates **the significance** of the **main point** and the supporting material.

3

This version is not perfect. For example, as you probably noticed, the fifth unit is not a correct sentence. A first draft doesn't have to be perfect, however. It just has to be a complete version, a document that holds promise. You'll fulfill that promise in the next stage of the writing, during which you will **revise** and **edit** to create your **final draft.**

MASTERY EXERCISE 5 Evaluating a First Draft

1. Consider the first draft on page 25 again. In your view, what is the strongest part of the writing? What makes it stand out?
2. First drafts are never perfect. Rather, they are starting points for revision. As you see it, what is the least effective part of this paragraph? What would you suggest to improve that element?

Summary Exercise

1. For Mastery Exercise 2 (page 20), you developed a draft main point and generated some potential supporting ideas. Then for Mastery Exercises 3 and 4, you continued to build upon this initial material. Now, following the discussion and examples throughout the chapter, develop a rough draft of about 100–150 words. Or, if you'd prefer to start work on another essay, choose one of the following subjects, prewrite on it, and create a rough draft, using the examples in the chapter to guide you.

   - Facebook
   - a secret ambition
   - college versus your earlier educational experiences

2. First, review the material on amplifying to create reader-centered material (page 22). Then reread your rough draft. Put a checkmark next to the detail or example that is most reader centered, and circle any detail or example that needs to be more reader centered.

3. Take a break of at least several hours, and then scan your rough draft again. Underline or circle any obviously awkward or unclear spots and any noticeable errors in form. Also, make sure that the closing sentence restates the significance or importance of the main point and the supporting ideas.

4. Correcting any problem spots you have noted at this point, turn your rough draft into a first draft.

4

The Revising Stage

OVERVIEW

From First to Final Draft

You've worked your way through the composing stage of writing, and you've produced an acceptable first draft. But your work isn't over. Now it's time to turn something good into something even better, which you will accomplish through the third stage in the writing process: revision.

The word itself suggests what the stage involves. *Revision* is re-vision—seeing something again, with a fresh eye. It consists of three separate steps:

- reassessing
- redrafting
- editing

As you work through these steps, you'll identify strengths and find, address, and eliminate weaknesses. The result will be a final draft that is simple, clear, and correct.

4

The Process of Revision

To arrive at this point in the writing process, you first worked through the prewriting stage to generate ideas on a subject and then went on to composing to specify a focus—your main idea—and to develop supporting ideas and a closing sentence, all of which resulted in a complete first draft.

Take a look at the arrows in the following figure, which illustrates the writing process:

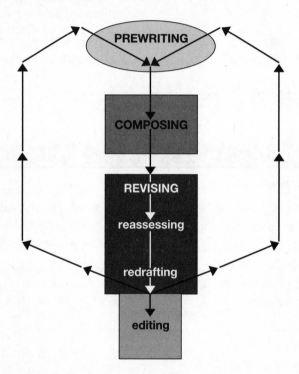

The arrows flow from prewriting to composing and on to revising. When you revise, you first **reassess** your first draft to identify what works in your writing and what still needs work.

Then you **redraft,** which involves generating new information to address the gaps and weaknesses in content. As you can see, the arrows flow from revising back to prewriting. The writing process is *recursive*—you move back through steps as often as necessary to create the most effective final draft possible. The arrows then continue back through composing and revising, leading you eventually to **editing.** The result is a polished draft.

4

Reassessing for Unity, Coherence, and Effective Language

After you've completed any job, it's a good idea to step back and look at what you've accomplished. Maybe you'll admire your work. Maybe you'll find fault with parts. Usually, however, you'll do both. Basically this is what you do when you reassess.

Take a day or so—longer if your deadline allows—in order to *create a distance,* and then examine your first draft closely. This distance is important. After all, when you completed your first draft, you made it as good as you could—at that moment. But when you have been away from the document for a while, you'll find it easier to be objective and identify both its good points and its weaknesses. In particular, you need to reassess your draft for

- unity
- coherence
- effective language

Unity

For your reader to understand your ideas fully, you must make sure that your writing is **unified.** In other words, all the supporting examples, illustrations, and details must be directly related to your main point. To maintain unity, you need to weed out anything that drifts away from the subject you are discussing.

Take a look at the italicized material in the following paragraph about dealing with a difficult personal experience:

I didn't always feel accepted by others because my family was poor. When I was in first grade, for example, Tommy Fleisher, the boy who sat next to me, used to make fun of my clothes, calling me "Dollar-Store kid." The teacher spoke with him about it several times, but he would still tease me when the teacher wasn't looking. *When Tommy was a sophomore in high school, he was arrested for breaking into a warehouse. Now he is studying to be a minister.* Other kids in class would make comments about my clothes, especially if I was wearing hand-me-downs from my brother that didn't quite fit right. The way

4

my classmates treated me made me feel different from the rest of them, something no kid wants to feel.

This material about Tommy in the italicized sentences concerns events that have nothing to do with the paragraph's main point. Eliminate these two sentences, and the paragraph will be unified.

MASTERY EXERCISE 1 Reassessing Unity

1. Read the following passage, identify the information that disrupts unity in the paragraph, and explain why you feel it doesn't fit:

   Tim's first mixed martial arts match didn't work out as he had hoped. In the first minute, a kick in the first round broke his nose. The blow knocked him back, and his arms dropped down. His opponent, an experienced MMA fighter named Jeremy Wright, took immediate advantage. When he isn't fighting, Wright is a doctoral student studying catfish. His research involves toxins that catfish use to keep predators from eating them. He advanced on Tim and used a combination of quick punches to knock him to the floor. In another 30 seconds, the match was over. In just two and a half minutes, Tim suffered a broken nose and a severely bruised ego.

2. Briefly explain how the remaining information in the paragraph provides support for the main point.

Coherence

An effective final draft must also be **coherent.** When writing is coherent, it makes sense, with each idea flowing smoothly to the next. The two basic elements of coherence are *transition* and *organization.*

Transition In order for a document to make sense to a reader, the relationships between ideas must be clear and obvious. **Transition,** words and expressions that show connections, provide

4

these all-important links. Two primary techniques help you provide transition:

- repeating key words and phrases and using *synonyms*—words with a similar meaning
- including transitional words or expressions.

To see how the first technique works, look at the italicized words and expressions in the following passage:

EXAMPLE: The *real estate developer* tried to convince the *city planning board* to allow *her* company to build homes around the *city reservoir*. The *board members* refused, saying the danger of polluting the *water supply* was too great a risk.

In the first sentence, *her* renames the *real estate developer*. In the second sentence, *board members* is used in place of the *city planning board* named in the first sentence. At the same time, the synonym *water supply* in the second sentence refers back to *city reservoir* in the first sentence. Using transition in this way ensures that ideas flow smoothly and eliminates needless repetition in phrasing.

The second technique involves using the following transitional expressions, which are grouped according to the types of relationships they indicate:

TO ILLUSTRATE OR SUGGEST CAUSE AND EFFECT

accordingly	consequently	if	overall
after all	for example	indeed	particularly
as a result	for instance	in fact	specifically
because	for one thing	of course	therefore
			thus

EXAMPLE: A job at a fast-food restaurant is harder than people think. *For one thing,* the pressure during meal times is enormous.

TO ADD, RESTATE, OR EMPHASIZE

again	finally	in conclusion	next
also	further	in other words	too
and	in addition	moreover	to sum up
besides			

4

Example: The number of overweight U.S. adults has continued to be a major health problem. *Moreover,* some health care experts refer to childhood obesity as an epidemic.

TO SHOW TIME OR PLACE

above	currently	once	to the right (left)
after	earlier	presently	under
as soon as	here	since	until
before	immediately	soon	when
below	lately	then	whenever
beyond	now	there	where

EXAMPLE: The deer stopped at the edge of the meadow, and *then* it bolted into the woods.

TO ILLUSTRATE OR SUGGEST, COMPARE OR CONTRAST

although	despite	likewise	though
and	even though	nevertheless	yet
as	however	on the other hand	
at the same time	in contrast	regardless	
but	in spite of	still	

EXAMPLE: The slope on the water slide seemed tame enough from a distance. Up close, *however,* it looked like the side of a cliff.

As the sample sentences demonstrate, these kinds of transitional words and phrases improve the flow of ideas.

MASTERY EXERCISE 2 Reassessing Coherence

1. Identify the transitions in the following paragraph. Make two lists, one of transitional expressions and the other of any synonyms, pronouns, or repeated words:

    My ride in a hot-air balloon was as amazing as I dreamed it would be. When the pilot, seven other passengers, and I climbed into the enormous basket, I could feel my heart beating like a piston. As the pilot fired up the heater, that propane device gave off an enormous Whoosh and within seconds, we were floating upward in the breezes. For the next 40 minutes, my companions and I drifted where the winds took us. Finally, the captain pulled a

4

cord, backed the flame back, and we descended, landing in a field. When I scrambled over the side of the basket and touched the ground, I knew I would never look at the sky the same way.

2. Take two of the synonyms and two of the transitional words or expressions you have identified and briefly explain how these words connect ideas in the paragraph.

Organization   You also need to reassess your writing for organization. Your goal is always to make it as easy as possible for your reader to understand your message. How you present your material plays an important role in this regard. Three common methods of organization are **chronological order, spatial order,** and **emphatic order,** and your specific subject determines which method you choose.

Chronological order refers to an organization based on time. Whenever your document involves presenting a series of events or episodes as they occurred, chronological order is appropriate. If you were writing about an annual holiday celebration, you might follow chronological order to present the details, as the following informal outline shows:

Main Point: Of all the holiday celebrations, my family and I enjoy our Fourth of July activities the most.

- *First,* we have a big cookout for about 50 people, including grandparents, aunts and uncles, and cousins.
- *After* lunch, we have an afternoon of co-ed volleyball and horseshoe matches.
- *Finally,* at 7 p.m., we all walk to nearby Washington Park for the big fireworks display.

Notice how the transitional words—*First, After, Finally*—indicate the sequence of events involved in the yearly party.

On occasion, you may need to provide additional background information for your reader, and in that case, you can use a *flashback,* an episode deliberately presented out of order. For example, if this year's celebration was especially significant because a family member's serious illness had led to canceling last year's party, you might briefly discuss those circumstances:

4

Flashback: Last year, many of us spent the day by the phone waiting for news about Gramma's emergency heart surgery instead of celebrating the Fourth, so this year's party was especially important to the family.

Spatial order refers to an organization based on the physical relationship or location of one element relative to another element. Whenever you need your reader to be able to visualize a scene, spatial order is appropriate. You explain or describe your subject in some logical, easy-to-follow way—from inside to out, back to front, top to bottom, left to right, and so on—to bring the scene into focus for your reader. If you were writing about the large lot where you used to play as a child having been gutted by a real estate developer, spatial order would help your reader make sense of the scene.

Take a look at this informal outline:

Main Point: The large wooded lot where my friends and I would play every day now looks like it was hit by a bomb.

- The large wild blueberry and raspberry bushes *close to the street* have been completely ripped up and shredded.

- *Next to* the huge granite boulders *along the right side of the property* was a huge pile of trees that had been bulldozed down, with the broken stumps pushed up out of the ground *across the center* of the site.

- The stream *at the back of the lot,* which used to be hidden by thick, green foliage, was completely exposed, with no sign of any of the birds and small creatures that used to live there.

Spatial order makes it easy to visualize the dramatic change in the area. Transitional expressions like *close to the street, Next to, along the right side of the property,* and *at the back of the lot* lead the reader from front to back, just as a person might actually walk through the scene.

Emphatic order refers to an organization based on importance or significance, which arranges the various supporting ideas and details so that they provide the most impact. This method of organization builds and maintains your reader's interest, from a strong supporting example or instance to a stronger one, saving your strongest example for last. You'll find emphatic order especially useful when you are expressing

4

a stand on a subject in order to persuade a reader. (See Chapter 13, "Argument," pages 105–117, for more on persuasive writing.)

Imagine you were writing in opposition to the practice of random surveillance filming of patrons at some professional sports arenas, casinos, and performing arts centers. Emphatic order would be the choice to arrange your supporting examples, as this informal outline shows:

Main Point: Owners of casinos, performing arts centers, and stadiums should not be allowed to install cameras to film people as they attend a performance or game.

- *For one thing,* this practice is an assault on personal privacy.

- *More important,* a corporation has no right to record a picture of you just because you purchased a ticket or paid admission.

- *Most important of all,* recorded images can be digitized and then sold or made part of some larger database, which could lead to abuse, especially if a company employs face-recognition technology.

Note the role of the transitional expressions *For one thing, More important,* and *Most important of all.* They stress the movement from strong example, to stronger example, and finally to the strongest example of all, sparking and sustaining the reader's interest.

MASTERY EXERCISE 3 Reassessing Order

1. Consider the following topics. Explain what method of organization—chronological order, spatial order, or emphatic order—you would be likely to employ for each and why you would make that choice:
   - A kindness that you'll always remember
   - A spectacular landscape or view you've seen
   - Limiting certain hits in high school football to reduce the risk of concussion
   - A frightening dream
   - Doubling the number of road lessons before taking a driving test
   - An event that inspired deep excitement or emotion on your part

4

2. Choose two of the topics for which you have already identified a likely order of organization, and do some prewriting to develop supporting details and examples. Then prepare main points and informal outlines like those on page 33, page 34, and page 35.

Effective Language

You also need to reassess the language you use. Phrasing that is vague, general, or insufficient doesn't communicate your meaning to your reader. Your goal is to employ language that is **clear, specific,** and **complete.**

An expression like *a nice car* may mean one thing to you, but it is very unlikely to mean the same thing to someone else unless you develop and explain it more fully. When you write "a 2012 electric blue Mini Cooper convertible with tricked-out chrome wheels," your reader may not agree with your assessment but will certainly know what you mean.

In some cases, you will need to include a clarifying phrase or illustration to help your reader understand what you mean. In these cases, you'll find the transitional expressions *for example* and *for instance* especially useful. The phrase *a hard job* doesn't mean much by itself, but when you add a clarifying expression, the result is clear, specific, and complete:

Clarified Language: Being a construction laborer was *a hard job.* **For example, the work day was ten grueling hours long, during which I did things like dig drainage ditches and push wheelbarrows full of wet, soupy concrete.**

Be sure also to keep your language **concise**—brief but to the point—by avoiding **deadwood,** language that adds no real meaning to your writing. This group of words includes intensifiers, such as *very, definitely, quite, really, extremely, somewhat,* and *a lot,* that add little meaning to your writing, especially in combination with general or subjective words. The difference between *warm* and *quite warm* is open to interpretation. A better choice is a more exact term like *sultry* or *stifling.*

Be on the lookout for any of the following deadwood expressions in the left column. Replace them with the concise versions in the right column:

4

Deadwood	Improved Version
due to the fact that	because
the majority of	most
has the ability to	can
in the near future	soon
prior to	before
completely eliminate	eliminate
come to the realization that	realize
with the exception of	except for
in order that	so
at the present time	now
take action	act
the month of October	October
give a summary of	summarize
mutual cooperation	cooperation
make an assumption	assume

Using the **active voice** rather than the **passive voice** will also help you keep your writing concise. Active voice means the subject is the doer of the action:

subject   verb
Active Voice: After the victory, the **coach congratulated** the team.

The passive voice means that the subject receives the action:

subject   verb
Passive Voice: After the victory, the **team was congratulated** by the coach.

Both versions are correct, but the active voice enables the reader to know right from the start—and in fewer words—who (the coach) did what (congratulated the team). The passive voice version is longer and less direct, in this case forcing the reader to wait until the end of the sentence to know who had congratulated the team.

4

MASTERY EXERCISE 4 Reassessing Language

1. The following phrases are not effective. Some are too general and nonspecific, and others are overly wordy. Revise them by restating them or adding information to make the phrases clear, specific, and concise:
   a. an interesting situation
   b. really, really cold
   c. extremely beyond the appointed time
   d. a serious thing
   e. give a summary of the group's informational gathering
   f. a damaged item of clothing
   g. somewhat not especially young
   h. the cute pet
   i. the fingers on your hands
   j. a very old piece of equipment

2. The following sentences are all in the passive voice. Rewrite them so that they are in the active voice, with the subjects doing the action stated in the verb. Then briefly explain which version of each sentence you think is more effective and why you feel this way:
   a. The successful surprise party was planned by my three best friends and me.
   b. The tired swimmer was saved from the riptide by the three lifeguards on duty.
   c. The stirring campaign speech was presented by a first-time candidate.
   d. The house fire was started by a little boy playing with matches.
   e. Classes for the day were canceled by the college president.

Help from an Objective Reader

Even with the flaws and weaknesses you discovered in your first draft when you reassessed it, the draft still makes sense to you. But the real test of your document is whether it makes sense to another person. If you haven't already done so, now is the time to ask someone else to reassess your first draft.

This reader could be a friend or family member. You might also team up with a classmate in your writing course so that each of you can reassess the other's writing. Just be sure that the person you select will be objective, honest, and fair. Someone who takes a fast look and says that everything is fine is no more useful to you than someone who takes a fast look and finds nothing good in the draft.

Ask your reader to use the following assessment checklist to evaluate your first draft:

READER ASSESSMENT CHECKLIST

❑ Does my main point clearly state the topic and focus?

❑ Do I stick to that focus all the way through?

❑ Are all my ideas and examples clearly connected and easy to follow?

❑ Is the language I've used clear, specific, complete, and concise?

❑ Does my closing sentence restate the significance of the main point and the supporting material?

❑ Are there any changes that you think I should make?

The answers to these questions will help you determine if your paper already communicates your good ideas to your reader or, if it doesn't, what adjustments you should make.

Here again is the first draft about a lack of self-confidence that was developed in the previous chapter:

My lack of self-confidence is keeping me from being as successful as I could be, especially in school. Most of the time, I am physically sick the night before assignments are due. Then there is the anxiety. I had to give a three-minute speech in American history last year, and it was bad. Have trouble with tests, too, especially essay tests. On my sociology exam last week, I couldn't complete two of the brief essay questions even though I knew the answers. I was just too nervous. I wish I knew a magic formula for self-confidence because I am sure my life would be better.

Here is a reader's evaluation of this draft based on the assessment checklist:

I think your first draft is good. I feel the same way about self-confidence—
I could use some more. The main point makes it clear what you are going to

4

*talk about, and the supporting examples you include are all related. I like your
closing sentence, too. If I had to make a suggestion, I'd say to explain some of
the examples more. Like the book says, they'd be better if they were amplified.
Also, I think you might have some kind of mistake in the fifth sentence—I read
it a couple of times and it still doesn't seem right. Already, the draft is pretty
good, and I think these changes could make it a lot better.*

With your reader's suggestions and your own reassessment completed, you are ready for the next step in revising: redrafting.

Redrafting

With what works and what still needs work in your first draft identified, you are ready to **redraft.** Your goal when you redraft is to make your draft more completely and more clearly fulfill its promise. To do that, you address the errors and problem spots that you and your reader have found in unity, coherence, and language, which, as page 28 illustrates, often means moving back through the first stages of the writing process to generate new information so that you can *amplify* what you have written.

Take another look at this brief passage from the first draft on self-confidence, which is not as specific and complete as it could be:

Vague and Incomplete: Then there is the anxiety. I had to give a three-minute speech in American history last year, and it was bad.

Now consider the same passage after redrafting:

Amplified and Improved: Worse, the anxiety is almost overpowering. I had to give a three-minute speech in American history last year, and I was dripping with sweat the whole time. It felt like an hour.

This passage is clearly better, thanks to specific details like the overwhelming nature of the anxiety and the heavy perspiration as well as the new sentence about how long the experience seemed to last. In addition, the use of a stronger transitional word—*Worse* instead of *Then*—emphasizes how upsetting the entire experience was.

4

MASTERY EXERCISE 5 Using Redrafting to Improve a Draft

1. In their current form, the following sentences are too limited to be effective. Amplify them by adding specific details and examples in the form of a complete sentence or two, after the transitional expressions *for example* or *for instance*.
   a. The change in the apartment after the renovations was amazing. For example, _____.
   b. The scene of the accident was chaotic. For instance, _____.
   c. The sudden thunderstorm disrupted all our plans for the afternoon. For example, _____.
   d. The meal at the new restaurant was memorable. For instance, _____.
   e. The final play of the game shocked just about everyone. For example, _____.

2. Using the Reader Assessment Checklist on page 39, evaluate the following brief passage.

> Many of the things that we use every day are adding to the growing environmental problems in the world. Our current practices don't affect us for just the present, either. Even if we started to act more responsibly, the problems would linger for a long, long time. A few simple steps could change everything. We owe it to the generations that follow to do something positive.

Now, using the sample peer response on pages 39–40 as a guide, write a brief note (100–105 words) to the writer indicating what you see as the strengths of this passage and what changes you would suggest to help the writer improve it.

Editing

The last part of revision is **editing.** During this step, you concentrate in particular on form, eliminating errors in spelling, punctuation, grammar, and usage. It is likely that you identified and corrected obvious errors in form as you were creating your first draft. Now, before you submit your final draft, you need to do one more close reading, called **proofreading,** to make sure no errors in form remain.

Be sure that you are well rested and free from distractions when you proofread. Otherwise you may miss errors, making your final

4

draft less effective than it could be. Use the following **Proofreading Checklist,** which lists a number of common errors in form along with the abbreviations commonly used to identify these problems:

PROOFREADING CHECKLIST

❏   Have I eliminated all sentence fragments (*frag*)?

❏   Have I eliminated all comma splices (*cs*)?

❏   Have I eliminated all run-on sentences (*rs*)?

❏   Is the spelling (*sp*) correct throughout?

❏   Is the verb tense (*t*) correct throughout?

❏   Do all subjects agree with their verbs (*s/v agr*)?

❏   Do all pronouns agree with their antecedents (*pro/ant agr*)?

Work through the list systematically, checking each sentence of your document. Adapt the list to match your own needs. If you find you don't have difficulty with an item on the list, cross it out. If you discover that you are prone to an error not on the list—for instance, irregular verb or apostrophe use—add it.

Have someone else proofread your final draft, too, perhaps a classmate who will serve as a proofreading partner. You can help each other by checking each other's work for errors in form.

You should also take advantage of spelling- and grammar-checking features on your computer. However, don't rely on these tools alone. Computers don't reason like people. If you type *clam* when you mean *calm,* these editing tools may not catch the error because even though these words have vastly different meanings, they can both function in the same way in a sentence. Also, these tools sometimes miss fragments and comma splices and occasionally suggest that correct sentences are incorrect. To make sure that all errors have been eliminated, *always* proofread your paper one more time after using these computer tools.

If you use the proofreading list to examine the first draft on self-confidence (page 39), you'll discover that the fifth sentence isn't a sentence at all. It's actually a fragment—it has a verb but no subject:

Verb Fragment: *Have* trouble with tests, too, especially essay tests.

To correct this error and change the fragment into a complete sentence, simply add a subject, as this version shows:

4

subject verb
Sentence: **I have** trouble with tests, too, especially essay tests.

MASTERY EXERCISE 6 Correcting Errors through Proofreading

1. Take another look at the proofreading checklist (page 42). Which of the errors listed gives you the most trouble? Why do you think you have more trouble with this error than with the others on this list?
2. Using the Proofreading Checklist, evaluate the following passage. Circle or underline the errors and then write a correct version above the incorrect one.

> Long before the sky grew dark on that summer afternoon, the oder of dust was in the air, the scent was peculiar, sharp and sweet, like dried hay. Its always the first indicator of a thunderstorm. I was suddenly aware that the air temperature, which has been in the 90s, were dropping so that my warm, damp clothes felt strangely cold. As if they'd been stored deep in someone's cellar. Suddenly, the biggest lightning bolt that I had ever seen flashed across the sky. A huge thunderclap that seemed to shake the skyscrapers along Fifth Avenue follows. Finally, with a hiss that grew louder by the second, the rain began. In a matter of minutes, their were puddles everywhere.

Check your answers against the corrected version on page 45.

The Final Draft

If you follow the steps outlined in this chapter to revise your paper, what happens? Here is the final draft of the writing on the

4

consequences of a lack of self-confidence, with highlighting and annotations that indicate the changes and improvements:

Note the addition of a title, which suggests the focus of the writing.

Self-Confidence: A Crucial Element for Success in School

The amplified details and more specific phrasing make the supporting examples clearer and more complete for the reader.

Careful proofreading has lead to the addition of a subject in the sixth unit, which transforms it from a fragment to a complete sentence, eliminating a serious error in form.

My lack of self-confidence is keeping me from being as successful as I could be, especially in school. Most of the time, I am so afraid that I'm not going to do well on an assignment of some kind that I'm physically sick the night before it's due. Worse, the anxiety is almost overpowering. I had to give a three-minute speech in American history last year, and I was dripping with sweat the whole time. It felt like an hour. But worst of all, I have trouble with tests, especially essay tests. On my sociology exam last week, I couldn't complete two of the brief essay questions even though I knew the answers. I was just too nervous. I wish I knew a magic formula for self-confidence because I am sure my life would be better.

The use of the transitional expressions **Worse,** and **But worst of all** stress the increasing significance of these supporting examples.

Keep in mind that making your writing as good as it can be will probably involve completing multiple drafts. But as this final draft shows, the hard work involved in revision is always worth it.

Summary Exercise

1. For the Summary Exercise at the end of Chapter 3 (page 26), you created a rough draft and then a first draft of about 100–150 words on one of the topics presented. Now, using the material in this chapter to guide you, it's time to revise that first

4

draft. If you prefer to develop another first draft for this exercise, choose one of the following topics and develop a writing of about 100–150 words:

- a positive role model
- what you dislike about Facebook or another social networking site
- whether some government agency should monitor the Internet and block discussions and information on certain topics

2. Using the material in this chapter as a guide, reassess your first draft, considering its unity, coherence (including transitions and order of presentation), and language.

3. Ask an objective reader, perhaps a classmate who is also working on a draft, to use the Reader Assessment Checklist (page 39), to evaluate your first draft.

4. After carefully considering your own and your reader's assessment of your first draft, redraft to address problem spots.

5. Check your draft for any remaining errors in form, using the Proofreading Checklist (page 42) as a guide. Ask another reader to proofread your draft as well.

6. Take a break of a day or so to create distance, and then prepare a simple, clear, and correct final draft.

CORRECTED VERSION OF MASTERY EXERCISE 6

Correcting Errors through Proofreading, page 43.

Long before the sky grew dark on that summer afternoon, the
sp (odor)   *cs (...air. The....)*
~~order~~ of dust was in ~~the air, the~~ scent was peculiar, sharp and sweet,
sp (It's)
like dried hay. ~~Its~~ always the first indicator of a thunderstorm. I was

suddenly aware that the air temperature, which has been in the 90s,
subj/verb agr (was)
~~were~~ dropping so that my warm, damp clothes felt strangely cold.
frag (...cold, as if they'd....)
~~As if they'd been stored deep in someone's cellar.~~ Suddenly, the

biggest lightning bolt that I had ever seen flashed across the sky.
Pro/ant agr (...all the people to hold their ears)
A huge thunderclap that caused ~~everyone to hold their ears~~
v t (followed)
~~follows.~~ Finally, with a hiss that grew louder by the second, the rain
sp (there)
began. In a matter of minutes, ~~their~~ were puddles everywhere.

PART II

The Modes: The Organizational Strategies and Approaches

5

Narration

Telling the Story

Whenever you write about an experience, relating the sequence of events or incidents that comprise it, the organizing strategy you turn to is **narration.** This mode enables you to focus on the key moments that will help your reader understand the event's importance or significance. It draws the reader into the experience by creating a sense of involvement.

If you wanted to discuss a violent argument you witnessed, for example, or tell the story of a time when you had to break some bad news to someone, narration would be your choice. To get the most out of this organizing strategy, you need to consider the elements of effective narration, including

- an effective point of view
- a thorough presentation
- appropriate flashbacks and flashforwards
- chronological order and sufficient transition

A focus on these elements will help ensure that your narrative writing is simple, clear, and correct.

5

An Effective Point of View

The perspective from which you present information is known as **point of view.** The *first-person point of view* is your vantage point as a participant, for example, if you were writing about a disastrous date you went on. With first person, you will use the personal pronouns *I, me, my,* and *mine* as you discuss your actions.

The *third-person point of view* refers to the vantage point of an observer of others. Third-person point of view would be the proper choice if you were writing about an incident of road rage that you witnessed. The focus is on others with third-person narration, so you will use pronouns like *she, her, he, him, they, them,* and so on.

A Thorough Presentation

With narration, you need to consider two important, interrelated objectives: providing sufficient information and staying on-topic. You fulfill these two goals by concentrating on what you want to communicate about your main point.

If you were writing about your misadventures during your first day at work as a dietary aide at an area hospital, your goal would be to communicate to your reader that little seemed to go well that day:

Main Point: From the moment I punched in five minutes late that first morning, everything that could go wrong did.

It would make sense to detail the different complications. You might talk about the food cart that you tipped, knocking several prepared meals to the floor. You might discuss your embarrassment when you delivered the first five meals to the wrong patients. You might also describe your mistake of getting on the wrong elevator and traveling down the wrong corridor, ending up in the wrong department of the hospital.

But including information about previous jobs or about your uncle the X-ray technician would not make sense. These details would take you off-topic and simply confuse your reader. Therefore, make sure to provide enough examples to make the situation clear for your reader without deviating from your main idea and getting offtrack.

Appropriate Flashbacks and Flashforwards

Flashbacks and **flashforwards** are devices that you can use to intentionally interrupt the flow of a narrative. A flashback is an episode that

5

occurred before the primary event in your narration, and a flashforward is an incident that occurred after the experience you are relating. An appropriate flashback or flashforward can give your reader insight about the episode.

If you were writing about the time you were stopped by the police at a speed trap and then discovered that your wallet, which contained your license, was missing, a flashback would help your reader more clearly envision the event:

Flashback: Then I remembered that I had taken my credit card out to make an online purchase and left my wallet on the desk next to my computer.

If you were relating the time a couple of months ago when you woke up to discover a spider crawling on the outside of your ear, a flashforward would help explain the incident:

Flashforward: But last week, when I jumped up because I thought I felt a spider web and knocked over a table in front of my friends, I knew I was not over my earlier encounter with that spider.

This flashforward would help your reader understand the long-term effects of the earlier event.

Chronological Order and Sufficient Transition

With narration, **chronological order** is often the ideal method of arrangement to present your ideas to your reader. That's because chronological order, as Chapter 4 explains (pages 33–34), involves presenting a series of events as they actually occurred, one after the other. As a result, your reader can more easily follow and understand the significance of the entire episode.

As you are using narration, you will find the following transitional expressions particularly useful:

after	during	later	soon
before	first (second, etc.)	meanwhile	then

A Narration Checklist

Once you complete a narrative draft, use the following **Narration Checklist** to evaluate it, and then ask an objective reader to do the same.

NARRATION CHECKLIST

❏   Is the point of view—first or third person—appropriate for and consistent with the document's purpose?

❏   Does the opening set the scene for the sequence of events to follow?

❏   Does the document supply a sufficient number of examples and details to keep an audience engaged without becoming sidetracked?

❏   Are flashbacks and flashforwards provided whenever information occurring outside the primary sequence is needed?

❏   Is chronological order employed to make the sequence of events clear for the reader?

❏   Is there sufficient effective transition to guide the reader?

Use the answers to these questions to revise and create an effective final draft.

An Annotated Narrative Writing

Take a look at the following narrative writing. The annotations point out key features:

Being the Bearer of Bad News

This **main point** prepares the reader for the episode to follow.

The hardest conversation I can ever remember having is the afternoon that I had to tell my mother that her godfather had died.
My mother was out shopping and had forgotten to take her phone. Someone in the area hospital emergency room called about

Note that the event is related from the **first-person point of view**—the writer as a participant.

an hour after she left the house. The woman asked to speak with my mother, and when I explained that she was out without her phone, she asked if I could track her down. Her Uncle Pete had been hit by a car near

5

his senior citizen apartment complex and had died, and my mother was listed as his next of kin. I told the woman that I would contact my mother and make sure she got to the hospital, and I immediately drove to the mall. After looking through three of her favorite stores, I found her. When she saw me standing in front of her, she looked at me as if she knew I had bad news for her. "Ma, the hospital just called," I blurted out. "Uncle Pete was hit by a car and died." I was definitely not prepared for what happened next. My mother, whom I had never even seen shed a tear, collapsed on my shoulder and started crying loudly. For the next couple of minutes, I had to support her. At last, she stood up straight, wiped her eyes, and asked me to drive her to the hospital. On the way, she didn't say a word. She just kept shaking her head. **It was the worst conversation I ever had, and I hope that I never experience anything like it again.**

The episode is presented in **chronological order,** with the series of events discussed in the order in which they occurred on that day.

The discussion is **thorough,** with numerous solid supporting examples and details.

Note how the closing sentence repeats the significance of the main point and the supporting information.

PUTTING NARRATION TO WORK

Choose one of the following topics and create a narrative of about 100–150 words. Use the annotated writing as a model.

A. What is the worst—or best—conversation you have ever had? For this assignment, put narration to work in order to tell your reader that story in full detail.

5

B. Most people would agree that online conversations are vastly different from face-to-face conversations. What was the strangest, funniest, or most unusual conversation you have ever had through e-mail or on Facebook or some other social networking site? Use narration to explain to your reader what happened.

FOR ADDITIONAL CONSIDERATION

1. Prewrite on one of the following topics, revisiting the events involved in that episode:
   - an accident or traumatic event that you experienced or witnessed
   - a time when you became lost
   - a time when you challenged authority
2. Create a draft of about 100–150 words in which you use narration to discuss the various stages involved in the event.
3. Using the Narration Checklist (page 51) as a guide, revise your draft. Make sure that the opening sets the scene for the sequence of events to follow and that you have included multiple examples and details that don't deviate from your main point. In addition, check that you have included appropriate flashbacks or flashforwards, followed chronological order, and provided sufficient transition to keep your ideas flowing. Finally, be sure to have an objective reader evaluate your draft in terms of these points.
4. Addressing any problems you and your reader have identified, create a final draft.

6

Description

Bringing It into Focus

When your goal is to re-create a subject—a scene, a situation, an experience, even a person—for your reader, the mode you need is **description.** With description, you draw on your five senses to capture perceptions and reactions. This mode animates subjects, abstract or concrete, making situations, impressions, and sensations almost tangible for your reader.

If you wanted to write about a childhood visit to the emergency room, description would help you express the fear mixed with fascination that the incident entailed. This organizing strategy would also enable you to capture the silent, colorful beauty you experienced while snorkeling along a coral reef. To make sure that you get the most from this mode, you need to consider the elements of effective description, including

- appropriate sensory details
- a focused and thoroughly developed presentation
- both objective and subjective description
- spatial order and sufficient transition

A focus on these elements will enable you to prepare a descriptive writing that is simple, clear, and correct.

Appropriate Sensory Details

Think about sitting down at a small restaurant somewhere and ordering a cup of coffee. What is the aroma like? What does the coffee look like against the side of the bone-colored mug? What does the mug filled with steaming hot liquid feel like? What is the sound as you blow across the surface to cool off the coffee? What does it taste like? To develop answers that will paint a clear picture for your reader, you need to focus on sensory details, the information you perceive through your five senses: smell, sight, touch, hearing, and taste.

Using concrete language is one way to communicate sensory experiences to your reader. To say that the container of milk left open in your car on a warm afternoon stunk doesn't tell your reader much. Words like *sour, putrid, rancid,* and *nauseating* do much more to communicate a sense of the sickening stench.

Comparing an unusual or unfamiliar sensory experience to something more ordinary or familiar is another good technique. Anyone who has dealt with a migraine knows that an expression like "a bad headache" is too general to capture the debilitating pain. Instead, you might describe it as *a ten-pound weight thumping against your temples and the base of your skull every time you move your head.*

A Focused and Thoroughly Developed Presentation

For your description to be effective, it needs to be focused. In other words, your main point should be clear and evident to your reader. It also needs to be thoroughly developed, with details and examples that communicate your meaning to your reader.

For example, if you wanted your reader to get a sense of the beauty you saw on a visit to the Grand Canyon, you would need to express this point directly:

Main Point: When it comes to beauty on an enormous scale, no scene has ever come close to what I saw when I leaned over the handrail and gazed across the South Rim of the Grand Canyon.

As you write, be sure to include only those details that are directly related to your main point. Details like the admission costs to the National Park or budget cuts that have reduced park staffing aren't connected to the beauty you witnessed, so leave out this kind of information.

6

Then, to make sure that your description is thoroughly developed, you need to anticipate your reader's questions, concerns, and interests relative to your topic and develop specific details and examples that address them. Your reader would likely be quite interested in what you saw and felt as you held onto the railing and looked across—and into—this extraordinary natural wonder. Examples like *towering red, purple, and yellow ridges and walls,* set against a *cloudless azure sky,* and the *green thread of the Colorado River a mile below* would help your reader stand at the edge of this natural wonder with you. So would details like the *searing heat from the noonday sun* and the *increased heartbeat* and *dizziness* you experienced as you stared down into the vastness of the canyon.

Both Objective and Subjective Description

Descriptive writing fits into one of two categories: **objective description** or **subjective description.** Objective description concerns actual and verifiable details, features, and qualities—matters of weight, size, color, and so on; and subjective description covers impressions and reactions that these characteristics and sensations evoke.

Consider a wooded lot in your city where you used to play as a child. It was a little less than an acre in total, with a large stand of mature oak trees, plus numerous pine trees and various bushes and other greenery. If you stood in the right spot, you could see through to the street on the other side.

But when you were seven years old, it might as well have been the Amazon rain forest. Once you entered, you were alone in your own jungle. It was as if the trees were as tall as mountains, and if you listened hard enough, you could hear the sounds of wild beasts.

The first paragraph about the wooded area is largely objective, covering the actual physical characteristics of the place. The second paragraph, however, is subjective, focusing on impressions, not facts. To communicate your main idea to your reader, you will likely use a combination of objective and subjective description.

Spatial Order and Sufficient Transition

With description, you will likely find spatial order the best method to arrange your ideas. Through spatial order, you explain the location of elements of the description in relation to each other, mimicking the movement of a person's gaze. You choose a starting point

6

and then move in a logical path—up and down, right to left, back to front, and so on—helping the reader visualize the details of the scene as they actually exist in relation to each other.

If you were writing about the aftermath of the worst flooding in your community in 100 years, spatial order would help you capture the scene of a small neighborhood next to a normally tiny stream. The backyards of the houses along the stream seemed more like a river or lake now. Swing sets, slides, gas grills, and even above-ground swimming pools were almost completely submerged. Water had poured into the first floor of most of the homes, some at least 100 yards from the stream. A small flock of ducks floated on the front porch of one house. This view, from the stream out to the street, makes it easy for your reader to comprehend the devastation.

As you use description, you will find the following transitional words especially helpful:

above, below	in front of, behind	toward, away
close, far	next to, near, between	up, down

A Description Checklist

Once you complete a descriptive draft, use the following **Description Checklist** to evaluate it, and then ask an objective reader to do the same.

DESCRIPTION CHECKLIST

❑ Are there appropriate sensory details to support the main point?

❑ Does the opening engage the reader and lay a clear foundation for the condition, phenomenon, or situation to be illustrated?

❑ Is the description fully developed and focused, anticipating audience interests, concerns, and questions?

❑ Are both objective and subjective description used at appropriate spots?

❑ Has spatial order been used to make the description easy for the reader to follow?

❑ Is there sufficient effective transition to guide the reader?

Use the answers to these questions to revise and create an effective final draft.

6   An Annotated Descriptive Writing

Take a look at the following descriptive writing. The annotations point out key features:

This **main idea engages the reader** and lays a clear foundation for the description that will follow.

My Little Window into the Ocean

Last summer, I had my first experience snorkeling in tropical waters, and what I saw only a few feet beneath the surface of the turquoise waters of the Caribbean astounded me.

Note how the combination of **objective** and **subjective** description helps bring the scene into focus.

In June, my cousin Jacqueline was married on St. John in the U.S. Virgin Islands, and a number of her family members went to her destination wedding. My sister, my parents, and I arrived in lush, green tropical St. John three days before the wedding to enjoy a

The different **sensory details**—the sense of claustrophobia, the sound of the breathing, the vibrant colors of the fish and the reef—enable the reader to gain a full sense of the scene.

little vacation, and on the second day we rented snorkeling equipment and headed to the white sand beaches in St. John. Just offshore was an impressive coral reef, and I quickly put on my mask, snorkel, and fins and practiced breathing in shallow water. Although I felt a little claustrophobic when I first put on the mask, I got used to hearing myself breathe and began to relax in ten minutes or so. Once I felt comfortable, I paddled out to the reef and I couldn't believe what I saw swimming along beneath me. Fifty or more yellow and black sunfish

6

Spatial order—
the location of
the reef and the
sea life—makes
it easier for
the reader to
follow the path
outlined and
visualize the
scene.

as large as my hand were darting here and there directly beneath me. A green sea turtle, moving with amazing grace, cruised off to the right, cutting through an enormous school of pale green fish. All around were hundreds of multicolored fish, nibbling on the bright reef. Just ahead of me was a two-foot fish that I immediately recognized from a photo I had seen earlier online. It was a barracuda, moving slowly as if it was trying to decide what to eat for lunch. **I don't think I'll ever forget that hour I spent just floating around and gazing through my little window into the ocean.**

This **closing sentence** restates the significance of the information in the main point and supporting ideas.

PUTTING DESCRIPTION TO WORK

Choose one of the following topics and develop a writing of about 100–150 words. Use the annotated writing as a model.

A. This writing recounts a vivid experience. How about you? What experience or situation in your life stands out for you as especially intense? Was it a severe weather experience, a ride on a huge roller coaster or other thrill ride, a scene at a concert or other performance, and so on? Let description help you capture and animate it for your reader.

B. Think back to the first time you visited a special or unique place—a big city, a National Park or famous landmark, a Halloween haunted house display, a college or professional sports stadium, etc. Drawing on the power of description, provide your impressions of this distinctive place.

6

FOR ADDITIONAL CONSIDERATION

1. Prewrite on one of the following topics, focusing in particular on the various descriptive details and examples involved:
   - your version of a perfect spring day
   - your favorite spot to get away and be by yourself
   - what you felt when you experienced a physical injury of some kind
2. Create a draft of about 100–150 words in which you use the various aspects of description to communicate the vivid and unique nature of your topic to your reader.
3. Using the Description Checklist (page 57) as a guide, revise your draft. Be sure you have included key sensory details and an engaging opening that gives your reader a clear foundation for the condition, phenomenon, or situation you are describing. Check that your overall presentation is focused and thorough, with appropriate objective and subjective description. Ensure that it is arranged in spatial order, with plenty of transition to guide your reader. Finally, be sure to have an objective reader evaluate your writing in terms of these points.
4. Addressing any problems you and your reader have identified, create a final draft.

7

Example

Offering an Illustration

Whenever you want your reader to understand a subject the way you understand it—by making it lucid and easy to follow—the mode of **example** is your answer. Through this organizing strategy, you clarify or back up a concept, situation, or condition. Example sheds light on the meaning or significance of a topic, fostering a greater understanding of it.

Example would help you explain different measures that elected officials could enact to improve the quality of life in your city or town. This organizing strategy would also be the ideal choice to discuss instances of bad driving you have witnessed. To get the most out of this mode, you need to consider the elements of effective example, including

- a clear direction with multiple supporting illustrations and details
- specific supporting illustrations and details
- relevant supporting illustrations and details
- effective arrangement and sufficient transition

When you focus on these elements, you ensure that your example writing will be simple, clear, and correct.

7

A Clear Direction with Multiple Supporting Illustrations and Details

Your reader isn't a mind reader. Therefore, to meet your reader's needs, you must provide a clear direction about your subject, expressing your main point in a simple, direct fashion. It's also your responsibility to provide a sufficient number of illustrations and details to support that main idea.

If you were going to write about common superstitions, this sentence would provide the kind of direction your reader needs:

Main Point: From Friday the 13th to lucky coins to cracks in a sidewalk, many people continue to let a belief in superstitions influence their daily behavior.

No formula dictates the exact number of examples you should offer as support. The overall length of the writing you are preparing is the primary determinant. In the case of the main idea above, three ideas are listed, which is a good number for a writing of 100–150 words. Just keep in mind that the more support you supply, the more likely you will be to communicate what you are saying to your reader.

Specific Supporting Illustrations and Details

Specific means "precise and exact." To make your point convincing to your reader, you need to provide supporting details and illustrations that are specific, not general. General examples offer only a vague or fuzzy view. It's not enough to *tell* your reader what you mean. You also need to *show* what you mean by making the details and illustrations you provide thorough and particular enough that they communicate their meaning to someone else.

The trick to doing so is to **amplify**—to provide information that bridges the gap of understanding between you and your reader. The *key questions,* the queries that journalists use to prepare news stories, can help you turn general illustrations and details into specific examples. Ask *Who?, What?, When?, Where?, Why?,* and *How?* about the ideas you want to include, and you will generate specific information.

A phrase like *a nice old house* tells your reader little. It is too vague and nonspecific But use the key questions to amplify that phrase, and you end up with something like this: *a 150-year-old two-story restored carriage house, with a slate roof and leaded-glass windows, painted in original Victorian colors.* An example like this gives your reader an image that is in far greater focus and therefore enhances communication.

Relevant Supporting Illustrations and Details

Your reader depends on you to include information that is appropriate and directly related to your main idea. In other words, your reader needs *relevant* supporting illustrations and details, ideas that are closely connected, commonplace, and easily understood.

If you were writing about habits that get in the way of improving your overall health, relevant examples would include *eating too much junk food, failing to follow a regular exercise regimen,* and *getting too little sleep*. But a detail like *spending almost an hour a day on Facebook* wouldn't be appropriate. An hour a day online would likely have little detrimental effect on your health. In fact, if participating in social networking helps to reduce stress or provides enjoyment, the time spent online might actually have a positive influence on your overall health.

Effective Arrangement and Sufficient Transition

With example, the arrangement you choose will depend on the significance of the supporting illustrations and details. In some cases, supporting points are about equal in importance, as would be the case with the writing about common superstitions (page 62). When this is the case, the best thing to do is experiment a bit, rearranging the order of the supporting ideas to see which order works best.

In other cases, some examples will hold more significance than the others. For instance, many health professionals point to a bad diet, especially one featuring excessive amounts of junk food, as a primary reason for bad health. Therefore, with the writing about impediments to maintaining good physical health (page 63), **emphatic order** would be a good strategy because this method of arrangement enables you to rank your examples from strong to stronger to strongest. Yes, failing to get enough sleep affects health, so it is a barrier to maintaining good health, and not exercising regularly is an even greater problem. But the biggest obstacle is consuming large quantities of food that is high in calories but low in nutritional value. Arranged in emphatic order, the supporting information attracts and then sustains the reader's interest.

With example, you will find the following transitional words and expressions especially useful:

after all	for instance	indeed	moreover	particularly
for example	in addition	in other words	of course	specifically

7

An Example Checklist

Once you complete an example draft, use the following **Example Checklist** to evaluate it, and then ask an objective reader to do the same.

EXAMPLE CHECKLIST

❏ Does the opening indicate the concept or principle that the illustrations and details will support?

❏ Are multiple illustrations and details provided as support for the main point?

❏ Are the supporting illustrations and details specific enough to clarify meaning?

❏ Are the supporting illustrations and details relevant—appropriate, commonplace, and directly related to your subject and purpose in writing?

❏ Has emphatic order or some other appropriate method of arrangement been employed?

❏ Is there sufficient effective transition to make it easy for your reader to follow the points you are making?

Use the answers to these questions to revise and create an effective final draft.

An Annotated Example Writing

Take a look at the following example writing. The annotations point out key features:

Bad to the Bone on the Road

The **main point** introduces the subject and prepares the reader for the supporting examples to follow.

    In the two years I have had my license, many of the drivers I've had to deal with must be among the worst in the state. For example, the number of drivers who don't seem to know how to work their directional signals is amazing. This morning, a driver on the highway suddenly pulled in front of me from the left lane without those directional lights blinking even once. I'm not sure if it's better to be behind someone driving around with a directional blinking away the whole time, so you never know if the car is actually going to turn or not. Then there are the aggressive drivers. They get within a few feet of your rear bumper, even on the highway, to try to bully you into driving faster or getting out of the way. Last week, one of these dangerous drivers pulled up behind a minivan containing several small children and began leaning on his horn, revving the engine, and yelling out the window at the young woman driving the van. But the worst drivers are the ones talking on the phone or sending or reading text messages. Even though studies show that driving while talking on the phone or texting is like driving drunk, this practice seems to be on the increase. For instance, last night, a car screeched to a stop two inches from my driver's side door. The young guy behind the wheel still had the phone in his hand. **Driving is already a dangerous activity, and bad drivers like these people put everybody on the roads at an even greater risk.**

All three supporting examples—drivers who fail to use directional signals correctly, drivers who are aggressive, and drivers who talk on the phone or text—are **specific** and **thorough,** conveying a clear meaning to the reader.

Each supporting example is **relevant**—directly connected to the subject of bad drivers and easily understood.

The supporting examples are presented in **emphatic order**, with the transitional word **worst** used to signal the ranking.

The closing statement reiterates the significance of the main point as well the supporting examples.

7

PUTTING EXAMPLE TO WORK

Choose one of the following topics and create a writing of about 100–150 words. Use the annotated writing as a model.

A. The complaints discussed in this writing only touch the surface of problems on our streets and highways. What are the worst examples of poor driving that you've witnessed? Or, if you'd prefer, what are your own worst driving habits? Put example to work to explain this bad roadway behavior.

B. Have you ever looked down a road somewhere and wondered what it would be like to just walk on or drive off to someplace unknown? For this assignment, use example to discuss a few places that, given the chance, you might travel to, and why.

FOR ADDITIONAL CONSIDERATION

1. Prewrite on one of the following topics, concentrating on specific and relevant instances and illustrations:
   - favorite weekend activities
   - entertaining advertisements
   - the best inventions or innovations of the 21st century
2. Create a draft of about 100–150 words in which you use example to explain and clarify your meaning for your reader.
3. Using the Example Checklist (page 64) as a guide, revise your draft. Make sure your opening indicates the principle to be supported and illustrated. In addition, check that you have enough strong examples to back up the concept you are discussing. Also, be sure that the examples themselves are both specific and relevant and that you have included enough transition to keep your ideas flowing smoothly. Finally, be sure that you have chosen an effective order of presentation for your examples. If the examples differ in significance, consider employing emphatic order to capture and hold your reader's attention. Remember to seek the assistance of an objective reader to evaluate your draft relative to these points.
4. Addressing any problems you and your reader have identified, create a final draft.

8

Process

Outlining the Steps

When you need to explain how to do something, how something is done or occurs, or how you did something, the organizing strategy of **process** is your answer. Process takes action or function and presents it in slow motion, simplifying complexity and making it easier for a reader to comprehend.

Process appears in three different forms. The most common type, *how-to writing,* is used to give directions, for instance, how to shoot a foul shot. The second type, *process analysis,* explains how some man-made or natural phenomenon—a tornado, for example—develops. The third type, *process narrative,* details how you did something, for instance, organized and directed a cleanup in a neglected city park. To make sure that you get the most out of this mode, you need to consider the elements of effective process, including

- a clear focus and simple, logical steps
- appropriate use of the imperative mood
- reasonable expectations and necessary cautions
- linear order and sufficient transition

These elements will help you create a process writing that is simple, clear, and correct.

67

8

A Clear Focus and Simple, Logical Steps

With process, you will generally be writing about a subject that you understand more than your reader does. The more complicated or technical the subject is, the greater the chance that your reader won't know much about it. To make it easier for your reader to come to understand the subject as you do, you need to specify your focus and then present the process itself in simple, logical steps.

If you were writing about a remarkable process like human vision, your main point should indicate your focus:

Main Point: Human vision is an intricate process that occurs because of the interactions of a number of highly adapted components.

With the focus stated, you could then approach the complexity involved by presenting it in four simple, logical steps:

1. Light enters the lens of the eye and strikes specialized photoreceptor cells known as *rods* and *cones* in the tissue at the back of the eye called the *retina*.
2. The light stimulates the photoreceptor cells to record the image within the range of the lens.
3. The photoreceptor cells send the visual message captured on the retina along the optic nerves to the vision center of the brain, the *visual cortex*.
4. The visual cortex translates the signals into a mental image.

Presented in this fashion, this complicated process is far easier for the average person to understand.

Appropriate Use of the Imperative Mood

Readers seek out process writing, especially sets of directions, in order to gain a better understanding of an unfamiliar procedure. Therefore, with how-to writing, it makes sense to address the reader directly by using the **imperative mood,** sometimes informally called the **command.** The subject in the imperative mood is not stated but is *understood* to be the person being directly addressed.

If you were writing about how to insert a contact lens for the first time, you might write

---

To insert a contact lens, the contact lens wearer should

take a lens from the package and rinse it thoroughly with contact lens solution. Next, the wearer should place the clean lens on the index finger of the wearer's dominant hand.

But it would be better to use the imperative mood and write

To insert a contact lens, take the lens from the package and rinse it thoroughly with contact lens solution. Next, place the clean lens on the index finger of your dominant hand.

Thanks to the use of the imperative mood, the passage is now shorter (32 words versus 41), and, more important, clearer and more direct.

Reasonable Expectations and Necessary Cautions

To make sure that your reader is wholly prepared for the process you are presenting, indicate reasonable expectations and offer appropriate cautions about potentially confusing steps or stages. If performing a particular move in kickboxing initially causes a pulling sensation in the hamstring that will dissipate over several weeks of practice, reassure your reader that the motion won't cause permanent damage. The use of negative space—the empty area between objects—in drawing and painting can be confusing for beginning artists. It's a good idea, then, to caution your reader to be patient, that while the concept can be hard to understand at first, practice will lead to mastery.

Linear Order and Sufficient Transition

With much process writing, **linear order** is the ideal method of arrangement. Linear order is a variation of chronological order through which the steps appear in their functional order—in a direct line, step by step, in the order that leads to completion.

A writing explaining how a coral reef forms would call for linear order.

- *First,* a coral larva attaches itself to some submerged hard surface near an island or other landform.

8

- *Then* this tiny animal draws limestone from the seawater to create a limestone skeleton, with the result called a coral polyp.
- *Meanwhile,* multiple other larvae implant nearby.
- *Finally,* over a period of hundreds of years, the resulting polyp colonies become coral reefs.

As you are using process, you will find the following transitional words especially useful:

Beginning	Continuing			Ending
begin by	as soon as	second step, etc.	until	finally
initially	next	then	while	last

A Process Checklist

Once you complete a process draft, use the following **Process Checklist** to evaluate it, and then ask an objective reader to do the same.

PROCESS CHECKLIST

❑ Does the opening identify the specific focus regarding the procedure or technique?

❑ Are the steps simple and logical, or should any step be divided or explained more fully?

❑ If it's appropriate, has the imperative mood (*you*) been used to address the reader directly?

❑ Have reasonable expectations and necessary cautions been included for potentially confusing steps or stages?

❑ Are the steps presented in linear order or some other appropriate method of arrangement?

❑ Is there sufficient effective transition to guide the reader?

Use the answers to these questions to revise and create an effective final draft.

An Annotated Process Writing

Take a look at the following process writing. The annotations point out key features:

Making Those Free Throws Count

This **main point** identifies the subject, spurring the interest of the reader by referring to superstar Shaquille O'Neal and his problems at the foul line.

→   **If you want to make sure that you don't end up with a reputation for missing foul shots like NBA center Shaquille O'Neal, follow these simple steps.** First, step up to the foul line, keeping the tips of your feet at least an inch back. If you can see both edges of the line when you look down, you are all set. Your dominant foot should be about

Because this is how-to writing, the **imperative mood**—the **command**—is used to present the steps of the process.

→ a half-step ahead of your other foot. Your dominant foot will be the opposite of your dominant hand. If you are right-handed like I am, your dominant foot is your left. Next, flex your knees a little, and dribble the ball a couple of times while staring at the top edge

The various steps are all **carefully** and **logically** laid out to make it easier for the reader to complete the process.

→ of the square behind the hoop. That's your target. At this point, grab the ball, spreading the fingers of your dominant hand across the top of the ball, with your fingertips along one of the seams. Now slide your other hand down the side of the ball a bit so that it is helping to support the ball. Pull the ball up

8

and arch your dominant hand back so that the ball is resting on your spread fingertips. Finally, bring your forearms toward your body and then push them away, releasing the ball toward the target. As you release the ball, push off with your fingertips, adding a backward spin. When your arms follow your eyes, the ball will hit the target, and the backspin will ensure that the result is all net, all the time. **If you practice these steps, it won't be long before you consistently pick up those points from the foul line, something Shaq's teammates often wish he would do.**

Transitional **words** and **expression**s— *first, next, at this point, now, finally*—signal the move from one step to the next, guiding the reader through the process.

This **closing sentence** emphasizes the **significance** of the steps while reiterating the focus expressed in the **main point**.

PUTTING PROCESS TO WORK

Choose one of the following topics and create a writing of about 100–150 words. Use the annotated writing as a model.

A. Think of any sport that you have played or followed closely. Choose one movement, step, play, or approach—for instance, putting in golf, serving in tennis, speeding over a high hurdle, throwing a football or javelin, and so on—and, using this example about shooting a foul shot as a model, use process to explain how to perform this action.

B. Did you ever make the big play in a game—or FAIL TO make the big play (or watch someone else succeed or fail in the attempt)? Use process to recount the series of steps that led to the thrill of victory or the agony of defeat.

8

FOR ADDITIONAL CONSIDERATION

1. Prewrite on one of the following topics, focusing on the steps or stages comprising it. Consult additional sources if necessary and correctly document any information you draw from these sources:
   - how an eclipse occurs
   - how to parallel park
   - how to upload a video clip to a Web page
2. Create a draft of about 100–150 words in which you identify for your reader the steps making up the process.
3. Using the Process Checklist (page 70) as a guide, revise your draft. Make sure that your opening sets a clear direction for your reader and that the process is divided into simple, logical steps. If appropriate, check that the imperative voice has been used, and that any necessary cautions or clarifications about difficult steps or stages have been provided. At the same time, be sure that linear order or some other suitable method of arrangement has been used, along with sufficient transition to keep your meaning flowing for your reader.
4. Addressing any problems you and your reader have identified, create a final draft.

9

Definition

Specifying Meaning

Successful communication on any subject depends on a common under-standing of the language used to discuss that subject. When you want to specify the characteristics or elements of some item, figure, quality, and so on, **definition** is the organizing strategy to choose. This mode estab-lishes borders around or distinctions among meanings for both abstract and concrete subjects, interpreting and translating them for your reader.

Through definition, you could explain what it means to be an intellec-tual. This organizing strategy would also enable you to explain what consti-tutes true maturity. To make sure that you get the most out of this mode, you need to consider the elements of effective definition, including

- a clear direction and the elements of an effective definition
- approaches to develop an extended definition
- appropriate personal interpretations or experiences
- effective arrangement and sufficient transition

Concentrating on these aspects will help you create a definition writing that is simple, clear, and correct.

A Clear Direction and the Elements of an Effective Definition

Before your reader can begin to comprehend your interpretation or understanding of a subject, you need to provide a clear direction through your main point. As you do so, draw on the basic pattern of a dictionary definition. This technique identifies the general class to which the term belongs and then gives the special or distinguishing characteristics that set the word apart, as this example shows:

class

EXAMPLE: An assault is a **criminal act** that involves an
distinguishing characteristics
attempted physical attack or threat to injure another.

This kind of starting point is called a *limited definition,* and you can use your main point to express it. For a subject like heroism, here's what this starting point would look like:

Main Point: Heroism is a special quality, which I believe is in everyone, that involves stepping beyond personal safety or comfort for the sole benefit of someone else.

With the main point expressed this way, your reader is prepared for the discussion about heroism to follow.

Approaches to Develop an Extended Definition

An *extended definition* is a fully developed explanation, complete with multiple supporting examples. A number of approaches can help you develop the details and illustrations that offer effective support for your definition, including

- **denotation and connotation**

  Denotation is the literal meaning of a word, and **connotation** refers to all the associations that accompany the word. The denotation of a simple word like *intense* is "forceful" or "existing to a high degree," but its connotations can suggest different meanings depending on how the word is used. When you say

9

that a child waiting to bat during a T-ball game is intense, you mean "eager" or "highly focused." But when you say that a guest speaker on human rights is intense, you mean "passionate" or "ardent" or "deeply committed." With definition, always consider both denotation and connotation to make sure that what you write reflects what you mean.

- **synonyms, negation, and etymology**

A **synonym,** a word that holds a similar meaning to another word, is an excellent way to specify your meaning. If you write that your friend is *meticulous* about personal appearance, synonyms like *fastidious* and *demanding* offer a more exact sense of how concerned he is about the image he projects.

With **negation,** you define something by explaining what it *isn't*. When you write, "Sexual harassment is not just making a joke with sexual overtones," you indicate that this problem is more complex than many people are aware.

Etymology refers to the origin and historical development of a word. An unabridged dictionary such as the *Oxford English Dictionary (OED)* is the best place to find extensive etymological information. A search engine can also take you to a number of online sites devoted to etymology. With such an online tool, you might learn that high school and college cross-country runners are often called *harriers*. This nickname comes from a breed of hounds used in packs to hunt for small animals like rabbits.

Appropriate Personal Interpretations or Experiences

You may find that including an appropriate personal interpretation or experience in your definition may heighten reader interest and clarify meaning. With an abstract subject like *anxiety*, explaining

your own experience with it could make it easier for your reader to
understand exactly what you mean:

For me, anxiety can be almost paralyzing. For instance,
last month at work we were all notified that we had to reapply
for our positions and have a half-hour interview with the Human
Resources Director. If the interview didn't go well, we could be
fired. I really need my job, so from the moment we were notified,
I developed nausea and a pounding headache, and I didn't stop
feeling sick until three weeks later, when I completed my interview
and was told I was rehired.

This recounted experience clearly shows the physical effects of
anxiety, so it offers solid support for the overall definition.

Effective Arrangement and Sufficient Transition

How you arrange your definition will help determine how easily your
reader is able to understand the meaning of the quality, characteristic,
feature, and so on, as you understand it. Your subject will influence
the order you employ.

Sometimes, how we understand a term evolves as a result of
different experiences. For example, your approach to defining a
topic like a *bad teammate* might be to explain your interactions with
an extremely talented but equally self-centered player on your high
school soccer team. In that case, you might use chronological order
to tell the story of a tournament loss the team suffered because of
this player's inability to act for the good of the team.

Often, however, the definitions that you will present have several
components or elements, with some more significant than others. In
such cases, emphatic order, the method of arrangement in which supporting material is ranked, would be the best choice. For instance, if
you were defining common courtesy, you might include discussions of
such behavior as holding a door for someone, excusing yourself if you
brush by someone, and being respectful to older people. But far more
important than these behaviors is refraining from having cell phone
conversations in restaurants and other public spaces. Arranged from

9

strong to stronger to strongest example, this definition of common courtesy feeds and holds the attention and interest of your reader.

The following transitional words and expressions will help you use definition to spell out the special qualities or elements constituting your subject:

| accordingly | in addition | in other words | on the whole | therefore |
| indeed | in fact | in the same way | specifically | thus |

A Definition Checklist

Once you complete a definition draft, use the following **Definition Checklist** to evaluate it. Then ask an objective reader to do the same.

DEFINITION CHECKLIST

❑ Does the opening clearly identify the term to be defined in the body?

❑ Does the main point include a limited definition?

❑ Have matters such as denotation and connotation been considered and strategies like the use of synonyms, negation, and etymology been employed to create an expanded definition?

❑ Have personal interpretations or experiences been included when appropriate?

❑ Has the material been presented in an effective order?

❑ Is there sufficient transition to guide the reader?

Use the answers to these questions to revise and create an effective final draft.

An Annotated Definition Writing

Take a look at the following definition writing. The annotations point out key features:

Maturity: Not Just a Matter of Age

Genuine maturity means not only

realizing that you have responsibilities to your

family, friends, instructors, and bosses but

9

The **main point** serves as a **limited definition** for responsibility, preparing the reader for the elements of definition to follow.

The supporting material includes examples of acting maturely, including fulfilling household duties, keeping promises and commitments to others, and attending to school and work commitments.

also acting on those responsibilities. If you have duties around the house, whether it is yard work or laundry or cooking, you need to get it done without anyone reminding or pestering you about it. Also, if you are mature, you always follow through on your commitments. If you've promised to take your younger siblings to the park or mall on a Saturday, you have to do it even if you get an offer from your friends to attend a last-minute barbeque. Your promise is your word. If you agree to help out with a charity activity on a summer afternoon, you show up and honor your obligation even though it would be nice to head off to the beach. A mature person sets an alarm clock to get up on time for work or school and makes sure to complete all assigned tasks or homework. **When you are truly mature, friends, family members, instructors, and supervisors know that they can depend on you because when you say you'll do something, it consistently gets done.**

Note that the supporting information consists of **appropriate personal interpretations and experiences**. In addition, **synonyms** for responsibility—*duties, commitments, promise, obligation*—help to clarify the definition.

The **closing sentence** restates the significance of the definition expressed in the main point and the supporting material.

9 **PUTTING DEFINITION TO WORK**

Choose one of the following topics and create a writing of about 100–150 words. Use the annotated writing as a model.

A. This writing offers a definition of *maturity*. How about its opposite, *immaturity:* How would you define this term? Consider the aspects of definition and offer your view of *immaturity*.

B. A mature person, as the definition writing indicates, follows through on commitments like helping out with a charity activity. But what is *charity,* as you understand it? Use the power of definition to explain what this abstract, subjective term means to you.

FOR ADDITIONAL CONSIDERATION

1. Prewrite on one of the following topics, identifying its specific characteristics:
   - a slob
   - a bad boss
   - a true sports, music, or movie fan
2. Create a draft of about 100–150 words in which you use definition to delineate in full detail the unique elements and qualities of your subject so that your reader understands it as you do.
3. Using the Definition Checklist (page 78) as a guide, revise your draft. Be sure your opening indicates a limited definition of your subject. Check that you have considered denotation and connotation and employed such expansion techniques as synonyms, negation, and etymology. At the same time, make sure that you have included appropriate personal interpretation or experiences. Finally, check that you have employed a suitable method of arrangement with sufficient transition throughout. Remember to seek the assistance of an objective reader to evaluate what you have written relative to these points.
4. Addressing any problems you and your reader have identified, create a final draft.

10

Comparison and Contrast

Examining Similarities and Differences

When your intent is to consider alternatives, identifying in what ways the chosen subjects are similar or different, the mode that will help you achieve this goal is **comparison and contrast.** With this organizing strategy, you cast one subject against another relative to a series of characteristics, attitudes, or elements in order to examine those features in each and then emphasize their significance or otherwise draw a conclusion about the subjects.

In your studies, you'll often find that you turn to comparison and contrast to deal with analytical writing tasks like essay questions, journal entries, and research papers focusing on parallel or competing literary characters, theories of personal development, management systems, and so on. This mode would also be the ideal choice for writing about the ways that identical twin classmates differ. To make sure that you get the most out of this mode, you need to consider the elements of effective comparison and contrast, including

- specific subjects and focus
- a clear basis of comparison or contrast

10

- a thorough and specific presentation
- an effective arrangement and sufficient transition

A focus on these elements will help you prepare a simple, clear, and correct comparison and contrast writing.

Specific Subjects and Focus

In order for your reader to gain a full understanding of the subjects you are comparing or contrasting, you need to provide a clear direction. To do so, you must specify the subjects and whether your focus is on similarities or differences.

If you wanted to examine competing Internet search engines, your main point would look something like this:

Main Point: When it comes to search engines, Google now faces a serious competitor in Microsoft's Bing, which offers some superior features sure to attract users.

With the main point expressed in this way, your reader knows right from the start that the subjects are the search engine giants Google and Bing and that the focus is on differences between them. As a result, your reader is prepared for the discussion to follow about features that distinguish newcomer Bing from the leader in this field, Google.

A Clear Basis of Comparison and Contrast

Once you have decided on your two subjects and your focus, you must specify the characteristics or elements to be examined. In other words, you need to establish your *basis of comparison or contrast*. It is certainly possible to use comparison and contrast to examine three or more subjects relative to each other. However, you'll likely find that an examination of two alternatives with common ground is more manageable for you and easier for your reader to follow.

Perhaps recent discussions about possible future manned missions to Mars have inspired you to write about the similarities between the Red Planet and Earth. The basic structural composition of both planets is the same—rock and metals—and both have days that last around 24 hours. Furthermore, both have similar surface geographical features like volcanoes, valleys, and polar ice caps and active weather systems.

Once you have established your basis of comparison or contrast, construct a planning chart like this one:

	Earth	**Mars**
Structural composition		
The length of a day		
Surface geographical features—volcanoes, valleys, polar caps, and weather systems		

This kind of chart will ensure that you include comparable information about each characteristic for each subject.

A Thorough and Specific Presentation

No rule governs how many qualities, features, characteristics, and so on, you should consider as you compare or contrast your subjects. Still, it's likely that you chose the subjects because you identified more than one or two points of similarity or difference. Therefore, to ensure that your presentation is thorough and specific, include at least three points of discussion.

If you were going to examine two popular smart phones, the iPhone and the Droid, you would likely discuss matters important to users such as the networks supporting the phones and available applications. But a discussion of just these two points would lead to an incomplete, ineffective analysis.

At the very least you should add a third point—for instance, cost, screen resolution, camera quality, or battery life. With the inclusion of a third point of discussion, the picture of the similarities or differences between these two devices will be far clearer for your reader.

An Effective Arrangement and Sufficient Transition

With comparison and contrast, you are focusing on more than one subject. To make sure that your reader is able to follow your line of reasoning about the two subjects, you need to choose an effective method of arrangement. Two options available to you are the **block method** and the **alternating method.**

With the block method, you discuss the elements or characteristics established in the basis of comparison or contrast for the first subject and then discuss the same elements or characteristics for the second subject. With the alternating method, you switch back and forth as you discuss each element or characteristic.

10

Maybe you have chosen to write about two teachers from your early school years. These teachers were quite different in terms of their ability to control a class, their overall temperament, and their skill at motivating students, so you've made these qualities your basis for contrast.

With the block method, you would discuss each of these qualities for the first teacher and then the same qualities in the same order for the second teacher, as this informal outline illustrates:

Block Method

Main Idea: Because of a transfer halfway through the year, I had two teachers for the second grade, and for several reasons, Mrs. Viveiros was superior to Mr. Hampshire.

Mrs. Viveiros
    Control of class
    Temperament
    Motivational skill

Mr. Hampshire
    Control of class
    Temperament
    Motivational skill

With the alternating method, you would first discuss the ability of Mrs. Viveiros to control a class and then the ability of Mr. Hampshire to control a class. Next, you would discuss the overall temperament of Mrs. Viveiros and then the overall temperament of Mr. Hampshire. Finally, you would discuss the ability of Mrs. Viveiros to motivate students and then the ability of Mr. Hampshire to motivate students. The following informal outline illustrates this order:

Alternating Method

Main Idea: Because of a transfer halfway through the year, I had two teachers for the second grade, and for several reasons, Mrs. Viveiros was superior to Mr. Hampshire.

Control of Class
    Mrs. Viveiros
    Mr. Hampshire

Temperament
    Mrs. Viveiros
    Mr. Hampshire

Motivational Skill
Mrs. Viveiros
Mr. Hampshire

As always, the method of arrangement that you should choose is the one that more effectively communicates your ideas, so you may want to prepare two versions and seek the opinion of an impartial reader regarding which order is more effective.

The following transitional expressions will be valuable when you write a comparison and contrast document. With similarities, consider the words and phrases listed under "Comparison," and with differences, consider the expressions listed under "Contrast."

Comparison		Contrast	
also	just as	although	however
both, neither	like	but	on the other hand
in the same way	similarly	in contrast	unlike

A Comparison and Contrast Checklist

Once you complete a comparison and contrast draft, use the following **Comparison and Contrast Checklist** to evaluate it. Then ask an objective reader to do the same.

COMPARISON AND CONTRAST CHECKLIST

❑ Does the main point specify the focus and the subjects to be compared or contrasted?

❑ Has a clear basis for comparison and contrast been established and followed?

❑ Has a thorough and specific presentation, involving at least three points of discussion, been provided?

❑ Has the method of arrangement that more effectively communicates the similarities or differences between the subjects—the block format or the alternating format—been employed?

❑ Is there sufficient transition to make it easy for a reader to make sense of the comparisons or contrasts presented?

Use the answers to these questions to revise and create an effective final draft.

10 An Annotated Comparison and Contrast Writing

Take a look at the following comparison and contrast writing. The annotations point out key features:

Identical and Yet So Different

This **main point** specifies the two subjects—identical twin sisters—and the focus on **contrast**.

A **clear basis of comparison and contrast** between the two sisters is established: music and fashion; choices relative to television and sports; and academic interests.

Two of my friends from high school are identical twins, but those of us who know them agree that physical appearance is the only thing identical about them. To strangers, Ava and Alena seem indistinguishable. But it doesn't take very long to find out how different they are. For example, their preferences in terms of music and fashion are miles apart. Ava loves pop music and all electronic music, especially anything for dance, and she loves high fashion. Alena's iPod is filled with classic rock tunes, and she practically lives in jeans and other casual clothes. In addition, they are different in terms of the shows they watch, including sports. Ava goes to Hulu and other sites on her computer to watch comedies like *30 Rock,* and she is a huge NFL fan, especially the Chicago Bears. Alena loves reality shows like *Dancing with the Stars,* and during football season, she heads to her room to read until the games are over. That's how uninterested she is in sports. The school subjects they prefer are

Three points of contrast are included, with supporting details, making the presentation **thorough and specific**.

The supporting examples are arranged on the basis of the **alternating method,** with Ava consistently discussed first and then Alena.

→ also not alike in the least. Ava loves math, especially calculus, and she plans to be a civil engineer. Literature and writing are Alena's favorites, and she is going to school to major in communications, with hopes to work in public relations someday. **Although my friends Ava and Alena are identical twins, in a number of ways they couldn't be more different.**

The **closing sentence** restates the significance of the main point and the supporting examples.

PUTTING COMPARISON AND CONTRAST TO WORK

Choose one of the following topics and create a writing of about 100–150 words. Use the annotated writing as a model.

A. Think of two friends or family members who are more alike— or more different—than people might think, and then use the power of comparison and contrast to describe them to your reader.

B. On the basis of your experiences so far, would you say that college is, for the most part, different from your previous educational experiences or more of the same? Decide where you stand on this issue, and use comparison or contrast to spell out the similarities or differences.

FOR ADDITIONAL CONSIDERATION

1. Prewrite on one of the following topics, focusing on similarities or differences that come to mind:
   • two popular video games
   • two rival rock groups, singers, athletes, television shows, or theme parks.
   • having a conversation online versus face-to-face
2. Create a draft of about 100–150 words in which you use comparison and contrast to examine one of the subjects in relation to the other and communicate your findings to your reader.
3. Using the Comparison and Contrast Checklist (page 85) as a

10

guide, revise your draft. Make sure that you include an effective opening that identifies your subjects and your focus. In addition, provide a clear basis for comparison or contrast as well as a thorough and specific presentation. Finally, ensure that you have chosen the more appropriate method of organization—the block method or the alternating method—and included sufficient transition throughout. Have an objective reader evaluate your draft in terms of these points as well.

4. Addressing any problems you and your reader have identified, create a final draft.

11

Cause and Effect

Understanding Reasons and Ramifications

When you need to explain what brought something about or what has happened as a consequence, the mode to use is **cause and effect.** *Cause* refers to what triggers or initiates an event, situation, or occurrence, and *effect* refers to an event's outcome or result. Through this organizing strategy, you can examine the often-complex relationships between an occurrence and what led up to it or happened because of it.

You would turn to cause and effect to write about how obesity has come to be such a problem here in the United States. This organizing strategy would also be a natural choice to explain how becoming lost as a child led to long-term changes in attitude and personality. To make sure that you get the most out of this mode, you need to consider the elements of effective cause and effect, including

- a clear direction and appropriate focus
- direct and related causes and effects
- multiple cause and effect situations
- an effective arrangement and sufficient transition

By concentrating on these elements, you will help ensure that you create a comparison and contrast writing that is simple, clear, and correct.

11 A Clear Direction and Appropriate Focus

With cause and effect, your exact focus—on cause, on effect, or on both cause and effect—depends on your subject and your goal. In any case, you need to make this focus—your main point—clear for your reader.

Sometimes your subject and goal will lead you to concentrate exclusively on cause, as would be the case if you were analyzing pollution in various waterways:

Main Point: Streams, rivers, or lakes can become seriously
              causes
              polluted as a result of the infiltration of a number of
              common toxic substances.

Other times, you will focus on effect alone, as you would with a writing about outsourcing, the practice of sending work to nations where the prevailing wage is far less than it is here in the United States:

Main Point: The choice by many companies to outsource work to
              effects
              developing nations has had a number of serious
              consequences.

In addition, sometimes your subject and goal will require you to examine both cause and effect, as you would if you were writing about more comprehensive driver education as the solution to poor and dangerous driving habits:
              effects
Main Point: But reducing the instances of bad and dangerous
              behavior behind the wheel on the part of new drivers
              won't occur until the legislature
              causes
              makes significant changes in the regulations governing
              drivers' education.

Your reader always depends on you to provide a clear direction, so be sure to express your specific focus—cause, effect, or cause and effect—in your main point.

Direct and Related Causes and Effects

Not all causes and effects have the same level of significance. Some are *direct,* and some are *related.* As you write, be sure to differentiate between them so that you don't overstate any of the relationships discussed.

Consider a local factory specializing in fabric for furniture and automobile seats that has announced it will be closing in six months. The direct cause for the closing is that its parent company has merged with its major competitor. The conglomerate doesn't need two factories to produce cloth, so it has chosen to close the older facility in your city. The direct effects are that 150 people will have jobs if they are willing to relocate to a state 600 miles away but that 300 workers will be out of good-paying jobs.

The related causes of the closing of the factory include increased competition from fabric-manufacturing companies in other countries as well as a dip in furniture and automobile sales. In addition, the city's plan for waterfront rejuvenation made the factory, with its riverfront location, a valuable piece of real estate to be converted into condominiums, artists' lofts, and small specialty shops.

Related effects include a spike in the number of people seeking counseling to deal with the trauma of sudden unemployment and a dramatic drop in patronage at several coffee shops and diners near the factory. Also, the local community college announced plans for worker-retraining programs.

With some related causes and effects, the relationships are not necessarily clear cut. In such cases, use appropriate qualifying language—for example, *might be, seems, appears, rarely, often, sometimes, maybe, perhaps, probably, seldom,* and so on. These kinds of words will enable you to allow for another possibility and help you avoid making a claim that you can't support. Consider the use of qualifying language in this sentence:

EXAMPLE: Lindsey's decision to cut her warm-up short **probably** led to the calf pull she suffered during the race.

Including *probably* indicates that while a change in routine was the likely reason for the injury, the injury may have occurred for other reasons as well.

Finally, don't confuse coincidence—an event or experience that occurs around the same time as another event or experience—with an actual cause and effect relationship. That your windshield wipers stopped working a day after you filled the wiper fluid reservoir does not mean that adding the fluid made the wipers fail. Yes, one thing occurred before the other, but no evidence exists to indicate that the first led to the second.

Multiple Cause and Effect Situations

A single cause may have more than one effect, and one effect may have several causes. With cause and effect writing, your job is to present relationships in their full complexity.

11

For example, your decision a few years ago to begin martial arts training had a number of outcomes—increased confidence, new friends, improved physical fitness, and so on. The improved achievement rate in a school previously labeled as chronically underperforming happened for several reasons, including a new language arts curriculum, additional teacher training, and a comprehensive after-school tutoring program.

Always examine your subject closely to avoid oversimplifying what led to the event or what has happened or will happen as a result of the event. Remember—it's the rare issue, situation, or condition that springs from a single cause or has a single effect.

An Effective Arrangement and Sufficient Transition

An effective arrangement will help you present a cause and effect relationship clearly and convincingly. The order you choose will depend on your subject.

Chronological order would be the best choice if you were discussing causes or consequences occurring over a period of time. You might explain how your best friend became a rabid soccer fan in this way:

- *First,* on a whim, he volunteered to help coach a youth soccer team and found he liked the game.
- *Next,* he joined a recreational soccer league and began to play once a week.
- He *then* began following the regional Major League Soccer team, attending several games during the season.
- *Finally,* the spectacle and intense action of the World Cup completely captivated him and convinced him to become a certified soccer official.

Spatial order would be your choice if you were tracing how an area experienced some kind of physical change. If you were going to discuss beach erosion after a severe winter storm, you could explain the scene from the water's edge back to the shoreline:

11

- At low tide, it was easy to see that the soft sand *where the water meets the beach* had been washed away, exposing the stones and rocks underneath.
- The windblown ocean had breached the dunes *just in front of the beach houses.*
- The foundations of several beach houses *behind the dunes* were now completely exposed, with staircases hanging three feet above the sand.

With many topics, especially subjects with multiple cause and effect relationships, *emphatic order* will be your choice. If you were writing about the consequences you recently suffered as a result of texting while driving, emphatic order would enable you to discuss the relative significance of the effects:

- While I was texting, I didn't notice a stop sign, and, to avoid an accident, I hit a curb, ruining a brand-new tire.
- Worse, I missed my entire morning shift at work because I had to wait for a tow truck to arrive.
- Even worse, a police car was nearby, and the officer gave me a ticket for $150!
- Worst of all, now I have to pay a $300 surcharge on my insurance for the next six years.

The following transitional expressions will be especially useful with cause and effect writing. If you focus on what leads to something, refer to the words listed under "Cause," and if your focus is on what happens as a result, consider the words listed under "Effect."

Cause		Effect	
because	since	as a result	if
cause	so that	consequently	therefore
reason	unless	effect	thus

11 A Cause and Effect Checklist

Once you complete a cause and effect draft, use the following **Cause and Effect Checklist** to evaluate it. Then ask an objective reader to do the same.

CAUSE AND EFFECT CHECKLIST

❑ Does the main point identify the subject and indicate the specific focus on cause or effect?

❑ Are direct causes and effects distinguished from related causes and effects, and are actual cause and effect relationships distinguished from simple coincidence?

❑ Has appropriate qualifying language (*might be, seems, appears, could, may*) been used to avoid overstating any relationship?

❑ Are multiple cause and effect relationships presented with enough examples and details to avoid oversimplification?

❑ Is the order of arrangement—chronological, spatial, or emphatic—appropriate to make all cause and effect relationships clear for your reader?

❑ Is there sufficient transition throughout to guide your reader through the cause and effect relationships?

Use the answers to these questions to revise and create an effective final draft.

An Annotated Cause and Effect Writing

Take a look at the following cause and effect writing. The annotations point out key features:

A Long Time Lost

The **main point** introduces the subject—becoming lost in an amusement park as a child—and the **focus on effects**.

   I trace my shyness and nervousness at being away from familiar areas to the time when I was five and I became lost for almost two hours in an amusement park. I was there with my parents and grandparents, and for some reason each of them thought that one

Multiple related causes—inability to remember specific details about the incident and a long-term lack of concentration are also included.

Note the use of **qualifying language**—like *probably, because,* and *could have developed*—to allow for the possibility that these behaviors resulted from some other cause.

of the others was with me. I've forgotten many of the details, probably because of the trauma. All I can remember is that for nearly two hours, I wandered around the park as if I was in shock. When my parents finally found me sitting on a bench near the park entrance, I couldn't even answer simple questions, and I stayed that way for months. My problems continued once school started the next fall. In class, I'd spend all my time worrying that I wouldn't be able to find my way home, even though I had walked the route many times, instead of paying attention to the teacher. Sometimes I wonder if my troubles concentrating could have developed because of the times when I was so occupied with making it home. When I got home after school, I would just go into my bedroom and sit on my bed, leaving the room only for meals. I felt safe there. When my parents wanted to take me out shopping or visiting, I'd get very nervous and stand right next to them the whole time. Even in line, I would hold onto my father's shirt. I looked strange, but I couldn't help it. **Being lost in that amusement park made me terrified of being far from home, and I am still struggling to overcome these effects.**

Several **direct effects**—troubles communicating, fears of being lost again, retreating to familiar places for comfort, and clinging to parents—are provided as support for the **main point.**

The **closing sentence** reemphasizes the significance of the main point and the supporting examples regarding the long-term effects of becoming lost as a child.

11

PUTTING CAUSE AND EFFECT TO WORK

Choose one of the following topics and develop a cause and effect writing of about 100–150 words. Use the annotated writing as a model.

A. When was the last time that you became lost for more than a few minutes? How did you come to be so far off course? What short-term or long-term consequences occurred as a result? With the sample paragraph about being lost to guide you, use cause and effect to examine this experience.

B. Readily available and relatively inexpensive GPS (Global Positioning System) devices mean that getting lost is a less common experience than ever before. In what other significant ways has today's technology transformed our world? Turn to the power of cause and effect to explore the impact—positive or negative—of technological innovations on everyday existence.

FOR ADDITIONAL CONSIDERATION

1. Prewrite on one of the following topics, concentrating on some inherent cause and effect relationship:
   - an accident that you were involved in or witnessed
   - your interest in music, athletics, a particular academic field, drama, computer gaming, and so on
   - a time when you experienced extreme embarrassment
2. Create a draft of about 100–150 words in which you explore and then explain to your reader what led to this event or situation or what happened as a result.
3. Using the Cause and Effect Checklist (page 94) as a guide, revise your draft. Make sure that you identify your subject and focus in the opening. At the same time, spell out all cause and effect relationships in full detail and in full complexity, and choose the method of arrangement—chronological, spatial, emphatic—that most effectively communicates your supporting information. Finally, remember to provide transition so that your reader is better able to understand the cause and effect relationships you have identified and presented. Be sure to have an objective reader evaluate your draft in terms of these points as well.
4. Addressing any problems you and your reader have identified, create a final draft.

12

Division and Classification

Considering Segments and Groupings

When you want to break down a complex subject in order to simplify it for your reader, the mode to choose is **division and classification.** This organizing strategy consists of two separate analytical strategies that enable you to examine the parts making up an entire subject in order to foster greater understanding. *Division* concerns separating a subject into its essential elements, and *classification* involves organizing ideas into groups or sections on the basis of common categories, traits, or attributes.

Division and classification would help you explain the duties involved in being a home health care aide. This mode would also be the approach to use to discuss types of alternative energy. To make sure that you get the most out of this mode, you need to consider the elements of effective division and classification, including

- specific focus and a logical basis for analysis
- a clear and consistent presentation
- distinct and complete elements
- an effective arrangement and sufficient transition

Focusing on these elements will enable you to create a division and classification writing that is simple, clear, and correct.

12 Specific Focus and a Logical Basis for Analysis

With division and classification, your goal is to enable your reader to understand a complex subject by presenting it in units, piece by piece. To achieve your goal, you need to identify your *specific focus*—on division or classification—and establish a *logical basis of analysis*.

If you decided to write about the sections of your city and the distinguishing characteristics of each portion, you could use your main point to prepare your reader for the information to come:

Main Point: Visitors to the city where I grew up find it easier to negotiate their way around once they understand that it consists of five sections, each of which is very different from the others.

You could then discuss each of the areas—Downstreet, Granite Rounds, Riverview, Poketown, and The Tracks—and explain the unique qualities that distinguish each section.

If you were writing about non-motorized boating, you could use your main point to express your subjects and focus:

Main Point: Amateur sailors have a number of ways to spend a warm spring day on an area lake or river, including kayaking, canoeing, and sailing, each carrying a different price tag and degree of difficulty.

Then you could discuss each of these types, noting the cost to purchase or rent the vessel and the training necessary to enjoy the activity safely.

A Clear and Consistent Presentation

To help your reader gain a full understanding of your overall message, you need to create a clear and consistent presentation of the component parts or classes you establish. *Clear* means that your reader can easily identify the elements of division and classification, and *consistent* means that each category or class receives the same general degree of coverage, with no unrelated categories.

To ensure that a writing about the great apes, the group of endangered animals with the closest genetic links to humans, is complete, you would need to identify the characteristics for each of the four primates in this group:

- chimpanzees
- orangutans
- gorillas
- bonobos

But you wouldn't include monkeys, baboons, or lemurs. Although these animals are also primates, they are not hominids and they have physical characteristics like tails that the great apes don't.

Distinct and Complete Elements

The elements or groupings that you develop with division and classification must also be distinct and complete elements. A *distinct* segment or category is one that is separate and different from the others, with little or no overlap or blending. A *complete* component or set is one that is expressed in full detail.

With a writing about the people you saw in the courthouse while you were on jury duty, you might be tempted to group them as *people in uniforms, professionally dressed people,* and *casually dressed people.* But these groups are neither complete nor distinct.

For one thing, some of the uniformed people are actually court employees, while others are prison guards, and still others are members of local or state police forces. Some of the professionally dressed people are lawyers, but some are other court employees, some are courthouse visitors or prospective jury members, and some may be defendants. Finally, some of the casually dressed people are friends and family members of crime victims or defendants, some are average citizens taking care of legal business—paying traffic fines, for instance—and some are people curious about a particular trial taking place.

Therefore, to make sure that the elements are distinct and complete, you should shift the focus a bit. With this topic, you could concentrate on people wearing uniforms:

- court officers
- correctional officers in charge of prisoner transfer
- city police officers
- state police officers

12

Or you could discuss members of the public present in the courthouse:

- people called for jury duty
- prospective witnesses for trials
- individuals paying traffic fines
- family and friends of victims of crimes and defendants

If you discuss each of these categories in detail, the result will be a presentation that is both distinct and complete.

An Effective Arrangement and Sufficient Transition

Whatever you write, the order you choose should best serve the purpose of your document. With division and classification, this guideline means arranging the parts or groupings so that they help your reader understand the complete subject.

For example, when you need your reader to understand the physical layout or structure of something, *spatial order* is the best choice, as it would be with a writing explaining the structure of a modern running shoe. Discussing the makeup of the three major parts—the *outer sole,* the impact-absorbing *midsole,* and the *upper,* the fabric that surrounds the upper part of the foot—makes it easy for the reader to understand the protection and support this type of footwear provides.

When your goal is to explain the sequence of a condition, situation, or event, *chronological order* is called for, as it would be if you were writing about a progressive condition like Huntington's disease. The symptoms of this condition, an incurable genetic disease that causes destruction of nerve cells in the brain, are more easily understood when they are presented in stages:

- *The early stage,* which includes difficulties with coordination, involuntary movements, confusion in thinking, irritability, and depression
- *The middle stage,* which includes increased problems with involuntary movements, weight loss, reasoning, speaking, and swallowing
- *The late stage,* which includes severe problems with swallowing and weight loss, rigidity, and physical debilitation so great as to create complete physical dependence

As this brief outline shows, the symptoms themselves are cumulative, with each stage building on the previous one, so chronological order makes it easier for your reader to understand the nature and ramifications of the disease.

Finally, if your subject involves several categories, some of which are more important or significant than the others, *emphatic order*—moving from strong or significant to stronger or more significant to strongest or most significant—is the ideal strategy. During the last presidential election, then-candidate Barack Obama was asked what kinds of music were on his iPod. If you were writing about the types of music on your own personal music player, emphatic order would enable you to communicate the artists or kinds of music that predominate in your own personal music library:

- some rap and hip-hop—Jay-Z and Kanye West
- a somewhat larger collection of classical music—Bach, Mozart, Vivaldi, Debussy, and Aaron Copland
- a sizable collection of '60s and '70s music—the Temptations, the Beatles, Stevie Wonder, Bob Dylan, Van Morrison, Carole King, and Earth, Wind, and Fire
- the largest collection, consisting of alternative and world artists—Tori Amos, R.E.M., Bob Marley, Enya, The Cranberries, Yusuf, Sarah Brightman, Santana, and Green Day

Presented in this way, these classes make it clear that you have a broad interest in music but that alternative and world artists stream through your earbuds more than any other group of artists.

When you use division and classification, the following transitional expressions will help you emphasize the elements or groups that make up your subject:

can be categorized (classified)   the first type (kind), second type, etc.
can be divided   the last category

12

A Division and Classification Checklist

Once you complete a draft, use the following **Division and Classification Checklist** to evaluate it. Then ask an objective reader to do
the same.

DIVISION AND CLASSIFICATION CHECKLIST

❏ Does the opening specify your focus—either division or
classification—and establish a logical basis of analysis?

❏ Is your presentation clear—readily apparent to your reader—
and consistent—featuring balanced coverage with no unrelated
categories?

❏ Have you made all elements distinct and complete?

❏ Have you chosen the most effective arrangement to communicate
your divisions or classifications to your reader?

❏ Is there sufficient transition throughout to guide your reader
through the elements or groupings presented?

Use the answers to these questions to revise and create an effective
final draft.

An Annotated Division and Classification Writing

Take a look at the following division and classification writing. The
annotations point out key features:

Powering the Future through
Alternative Energy

The **main point**
identifies the
subject—
alternative
energy—and
a logical focus
on **division**—
different types.

**Fossil fuels are ultimately limited
resources, so if we are going to have the
power we need for the future, we must
continue to harness alternative sources of
energy.** One type of alternative energy is
geothermal. This form of energy involves

12

The **presentation** is **clear**—easily understood—and **consistent**—all the categories are examples of alternative sources of energy.

tapping into and capturing the heat that naturally exists beneath the surface of the earth. A second type is biomass, which consists of incinerating readily available plant matter—including grasses, trees, and recovered wooden building supplies—and animal waste. A third type is wind energy. This form of alternative energy, with a history extending back to ancient windmills, continues to grow in popularity across the United States and around the world, with individual turbines and entire wind farms drawing energy every time a breeze blows. Another type of alternative energy with a link to the past is hydro, which involves directing moving water through generators to produce energy.

The supporting examples are **distinct**—each category is different from the others—and **complete**—with each explained in specific terms.

These supporting examples are arranged in **emphatic order,** from least to most familiar, to draw and hold the reader's interest.

A modern innovation is wave power, which involves drawing energy from the movement of ocean waves. But perhaps the alternative energy source the public knows best is solar power. With solar power, the unlimited glow of the sun is converted to energy through photovoltaic cells. **Fossil fuels are declining at an alarming rate, so if we want to make sure the lights don't go out, we had better continue to develop sources of alternative energy like these.**

This **closing sentence** restates the significance of the **main point** and the **supporting examples** of alternative energy sources.

12

PUTTING DIVISION AND CLASSIFICATION TO WORK

Choose one of the following topics and create a writing of about 100–150 words. Use the annotated writing as a model.

A. Some opponents of wind farms have described the alternative energy sites as blights upon the landscape. In your view, what outgrowths or consequences of our modern world clash with or otherwise disrupt the natural beauty of an area? For this assignment, discuss several kinds or classes of elements of progress that could be viewed as stains or blots on the environment.

B. Think of your closet: what different kinds, levels, or categories of clothing are waiting for you? For this assignment, use the power of division and classification to discuss your own personal mark on fashion.

FOR ADDITIONAL CONSIDERATION

1. Prewrite on one of the following topics, focusing on sections or groupings of the subject that you have chosen:
   - challenges facing college students
   - types of workers you've encountered
   - kinds of restaurants in your city or town
2. Create a draft of about 100–150 words in which you use division and classification to make the subject easier for your reader to understand.
3. Using the Division and Classification Checklist (page 102) as a guide, revise your draft. Evaluate your opening, ensuring that it specifies your focus—either division or classification—and establishes a logical basis of analysis. At the same time, check that you have maintained a consistent presentation and used distinct and complete elements or groupings. Finally, make sure that your use of transition and your order of arrangement are effective so that your division or classification analysis comes across clearly. Have an objective reader evaluate your draft using these criteria, too.
4. Addressing any problems you and your reader have identified, create a final draft.

13

Argument

Taking a Stand

When your intent is to convince your reader to accept your reasoning on a subject, **argument** is the approach you follow. Unlike narration, description, definition, and the rest of the organizing strategies presented in the previous eight chapters, argument is not a mode but an aim or *purpose*. With argument, you use a variety of modes to persuade your reader of the validity of your point of view. Mastering argument is important because as a student, a professional, and a private citizen, you will often have to present and support your stance on some issue.

If you want to assert that school systems should notify the parents of students whose health may be at risk due to obesity, for instance, the resulting writing would be an argument. So would a writing that maintains that texting while driving should be illegal. To create the most convincing argument possible, you should consider a number of points, including

- an explicit stance and reasonable tone
- a sufficient number of valid supporting ideas

13

- absolute language and common errors in logic to avoid
- emphatic order and sufficient transition

Focusing on these elements is important because they will help you develop an argument writing that is simple, clear, and correct.

An Explicit Stance and Reasonable Tone

With an argument paper, you need to state explicitly whether you are in favor of or against the issue you are discussing. This kind of direct statement of your main point prepares your reader for the line of reasoning you will be presenting.

Imagine that you were writing about a proposal in your community to do away with recess in elementary schools as a number of cities and towns across the country have done. You might initially react to the proposal in this way:

Faulty Main Point: A proposal to eliminate recess in all city schools is certainly controversial, with some parents, teachers, and administrators in favor and some opposed.

The problem here is that this sentence doesn't indicate a stance of any kind. True, it is a controversial proposal, but you haven't indicated what side of this hot-button issue you support.

To eliminate the problem, express your viewpoint about eliminating recess in direct terms. If you think it's a good idea, you could write this:

Effective Main Point: The proposal to eliminate recess in city elementary schools is a good idea because it will free up more time to concentrate on serious classroom matters.

If you are against the proposal, you could make your point this way:

Effective Main Point: City elementary schools should continue to have a daily recess period because of the positive impact such a break provides for students.

Because of the effective main point, your reader is prepared for the line of reasoning to follow, regardless of your stance.

13

As you express your main idea and supporting ideas, pay particular attention to your attitude or *tone*. To understand the importance of tone, consider spoken language. If someone describes a house or working area by saying, in an even and casual tone of voice, "Oh, it's great," you would be inclined to take the description as accurate, and as a result your impression would likely be positive. But if the same person said, "Oh, it's *great*" in a sarcastic or mocking manner, your impression would be quite different.

The same thing is true for your writing. The tone that you use to express your subject can affect how your point of view is judged. A haughty or patronizing tone may offend or alienate a reader. On the other hand, a sincere, respectful tone will encourage your reader to consider your stand.

For example, because you feel strongly about the need for elementary school students to have a recess period each day, you might be tempted to write something like this:

Faulty Main Point: You'd have to be stupid not to see that a recess period allows children to blow off steam as they play and to build their social skills.

The point about recess may be valid, but the tone in this sentence is insulting. It fails to take into account that some people may simply be unaware of the valuable purposes that a recess break can have for children in terms of their behavior and development.

Now take a look at this version:

Improved Main Point: Some people probably haven't considered that a recess period allows children to blow off steam as they play and to build their social skills.

This sentence expresses the same valid point, but it does so with an appropriate, respectful tone. As a result, someone who hadn't considered these points about recess may be more willing to accept the argument you are making.

A Sufficient Number of Valid Supporting Ideas

With a main idea that expresses a clear stance, you next need to offer support for your point of view. This means offering several valid supporting ideas, examples, and details.

13

Valid evidence is accurate and truthful and based on *facts*—verifiable truths. It's valid to say that your state's slow response to severe flooding means that its emergency agencies were not as prepared as they should have been. However, it's not valid to say that state agencies don't care about the affected citizens, unless you can provide demonstrable proof that the lack of a timely response was deliberate.

In terms of how much supporting information to include, there is no magic number. However, chances are that you would need to see at least three points about a controversial subject yourself before you would seriously consider the stance being raised. Your reader is no different, so in most cases, include at least three points.

Keep in mind that argument is not a mode but a strategy or aim to persuade your reader. To help you fulfill that aim, you use rhetorical modes like definition, narration, comparison and contrast, and so on. If you were writing a paper asserting that cities and towns should institute strict recycling regulations for all plastic, glass, and paper, a number of modes would help you make this point. You might use description to illustrate a typical landfill, with piles of materials that might have been reclaimed and transformed into something useful. You might use cause and effect to explain how a failure to recycle shortens landfill life spans, and you might use process to explain how municipalities could generate a profit through recycling. Whatever combination of modes helps you make your case is the correct choice.

A good approach to develop support for your argument is to make two lists. The first should contain ideas that support your stand, and the other should feature information expressing an opposing point of view. If you can refute or adapt any of these opposing points, you can turn the other side's argument to your advantage.

With the writing in favor of mandatory recycling, the following points would offer support for your stance:

- Valuable landfill space is being wasted on material that could be reclaimed.
- A failure to recycle means that precious natural resources must be used to create new items.
- Cities and towns are missing out on possible income from selling recyclables.

Here are some points opposing mandatory recycling:

- Separating recyclables from ordinary trash into individual bins for plastic, glass, and paper is messy and inconvenient for homeowners.
- The start-up costs to establish a recycling program would be prohibitive for some cities and towns.

Of these two points, the first is easier to counter and turn to your advantage:

> Putting aside recyclables may be a little inconvenient for homeowners, but the benefits to the environment far outweigh these minor complications.

This point now offers strong support for the stance in favor of recycling.

Should you include the opinions of experts to support your argument, you must acknowledge and document that information. The **Modern Language Association's (MLA)** guidelines require that you provide the author's last name and, when appropriate, the page number, in parentheses following any direct quotation, paraphrase, or summary you include as support. Then, at the end of the document, include a full citation under the heading **Work Cited** (or, if you've used more than one source, **Works Cited**):

> As a recent article suggests, the reasons humans sleep aren't as obvious as people might think. "Such studies suggest that memory consolidation may be one function of sleep" (Max 77).

Work Cited

Max, D. T. "The Secrets of Sleep." *National Geographic* May 2010: 74–93. Print.

Check with your college library or writing center or look online for official MLA guidelines concerning different types of documents.

Absolute Language and Common Errors in Logic to Avoid

To make sure you don't overstate your case, you should avoid using any **absolute language,** words like *never* and *always* that express a certainty. The problem is that with many situations—maybe most situations—it is often impossible to be completely certain about an outcome.

For example, to say that our legal system ensures that the guilty *never* escape punishment is too extreme. Unfortunately, as good and

13

fair as the U.S. courts are, guilty people sometimes face no punishment (and, even more distressing, innocent people sometimes face punishment for crimes they didn't commit). It's thus more accurate to say that guilty people *rarely* or *seldom* escape punishment. When you are tempted to use one of the following absolute terms in the left column, substitute the more moderate term in the right column, unless you know with complete certainty that the absolute term is appropriate:

Absolute Word	Moderate Substitute
all	most
always	frequently
every	many
never	rarely

As you write, also be sure to avoid the following common errors in logic, often referred to as *logical fallacies:*

Fallacy	Examples of Faulty Logic	Instead, Use Sound Logic
Argument *ad hominem* (Latin for "argument to the man")		
Attacking the person instead of sticking to the issue	Why should anyone pay attention to what Senator Scrags says about educational reform? Last year, he failed to pay over $200 in parking fines.	Respond to the opposing positions.
Bandwagon approach		
Urging acceptance because "everybody does it"	Taxpayers should pay for a new stadium for the Sox because everybody loves professional sports.	Cite objective, qualified authorities or statistics.
Begging the question		
Assuming as fact what must be proven	The collapse of the retaining wall next to the new office building is just further evidence that the builder doesn't care about the safety of people.	Provide relevant, documented evidence.

Fallacy	Examples of Faulty Logic	Instead, Use Sound Logic
Circular reasoning Restating your opinion and calling it a reason	That smart phone is the best choice because it is superior to competing devices.	Give real reasons.
Creating a red herring Diverting attention to an unimportant point	Maybe that player did use steroids and other illegal performance-enhancing drugs, but how about the unwillingness of his teammates to sign autographs?	Provide compelling evidence.
Either/or reasoning Suggesting only two alternatives even though many possibilities exist	We must either allow the police to stop and search cars randomly for weapons without a search warrant, or the crime rate will just continue to skyrocket.	Explore all relevant possibilities.
Hasty generalization Making an assumption based on insufficient evidence	I began a diet last week and I have lost only one pound, so it obviously doesn't work.	Base conclusions on many objective facts.
Non sequitur (Latin for "it does not follow") Coming to an incorrect conclusion in relation to the evidence	I have always had trouble understanding mathematics, so I am going to teach myself algebra and geometry.	Think through relationships using logic.
Oversimplification Wrongfully reducing a complex subject	Legalizing casino gambling will end all the area's financial problems.	State all important aspects; admit inconsistencies.
Post hoc, ergo propter hoc (Latin for "after this, therefore because of this") Assuming a cause and effect relationship between two events that occurred by coincidence	The man accused of attacking his neighbor with a tire iron had just finished playing an intense computer game; something in the game must have triggered the violence.	Check your thinking for irrational statements.

Find the logical fallacy in the following paragraph about a fee increase for college students:

I think the recently enacted $25 fee increase per semester here at the college should be reversed. For one thing, tuition and fees here are ten percent higher than what college students in three surrounding states pay. Also, last year the college cut services and didn't replace any of the faculty members who retired, so there already were fewer classes available this year. Furthermore, many students can just barely afford college now. They will have to choose between paying the extra $25 and buying groceries. It's time for college officials to find a way to deal with this deficit without putting the burden on students.

As you probably noted, the weakness in logic appears in the fifth sentence: "They will have to choose between paying the extra $25 and buying groceries." This sentence is an example of *either/or reasoning*. A fee increase of $25 per semester is a significant expense for some students, but going without groceries isn't the only alternative. The sentence should be eliminated or restated so that it offers other possible solutions. For instance, perhaps these students could borrow the money from a family member or friend, apply for additional financial aid, apply for a hardship waiver through the college, pay the bill over time instead of in one lump sum, and so on.

Emphatic Order and Sufficient Transition

With argument, the best way to arrange your ideas is in emphatic order. The initial points spark your reader's interest and then the subsequent examples feed that interest, thus cultivating acceptance of your point of view.

Take a look at the following informal outline for a writing supporting the resumption of manned space flights, with the supporting assertions arranged in emphatic order:

Main Point: The U.S. government should provide funding so that NASA can resume manned flights in space, including possible expeditions to the moon and Mars.

13

- Early manned missions helped us better understand the nature of space and led to significant technological advances.

- In the future, humans may exhaust resources here on earth or seek to establish a colony on the moon or another planet, so we need to learn as much as we can about the long-term effects of weightlessness and the extreme conditions of space.

- Most important of all, the need to challenge ourselves, explore, and discover is part of the human spirit, something that distinguishes us from all other creatures.

Closing Sentence: So in order to continue to learn more about the universe, to prepare for our future, and to continue to pursue our natural impulse to challenge and discover, the United States should provide funding for manned space flights.

The initial reason—that earlier manned space missions led to scientific discoveries and technological advances—is strong. Stronger still is the second reason, that manned space flights will help us prepare for possible expeditions to set up colonies elsewhere in the universe. But the third reason is the strongest: it is a part of human nature to mount challenges, to explore, and to discover.

As this outline shows, emphatic order is the ideal choice for an argument. The significance of the initial point creates interest, and then the subsequent examples build on that significance, helping to persuade the reader that the point of view expressed is valid and reasonable.

Transitional words and phrases can help guide your readers through your line of reasoning and highlight the emphatic order. You'll likely find the following expressions especially useful as you develop your argument writing.

To Establish Reasons	To Answer the Opposition	To Conclude
first (second, third, etc.)	some may say	therefore
most important	on the other hand	thus

13

An Argument Checklist

Once you complete an argument draft, use the following **Argument Checklist** to evaluate it. Then ask an objective reader to do the same.

ARGUMENT CHECKLIST

❑ Does the main point explicitly state the stance on the subject?

❑ Has an appropriate combination of modes been used to fulfill the purpose of persuading a reader?

❑ Are there sufficient examples and details to support the stance expressed?

❑ Is the tone reasonable, sincere, and serious, with moderate language in place of any inappropriate absolute terms?

❑ Have any logical fallacies been identified and eliminated?

❑ Has emphatic order been employed to capture and hold the reader's attention and to foster support for the reasoning within the document?

❑ Is there sufficient transition throughout to smooth the way from one supporting example to the next?

Use the answers to these questions to revise your document and create an effective final draft.

An Annotated Argument Writing

Take a look at the following argument writing. The annotations point out key features:

The Driver's Seat: A No-Text Zone

The main point explicitly states the stance—that texting while driving should not be allowed. → **Sending a text message is fast and easy, an unbelievably convenient way to stay in touch, but one place where nobody should ever text is while driving.** For one thing, safe driving requires that drivers have both hands on the steering wheel, but sending a

Note that the **tone** is respectful. Rather than attacking those who engage in this unsafe practice, it acknowledges the convenience of texting.

13

Notice how the **modes** of **example, cause and effect**, and **process** are used to make the case that texting while driving is dangerous.

text on many phones requires two hands. That means that drivers composing a text message won't have their hands on the wheel, which can lead to weaving in and out of lanes, endangering themselves and other drivers. Even if drivers position their phones so that they can use one hand to type the message, they still will likely have to get into an awkward position to do so. As a result, these drivers ultimately have less control over their cars than they need to drive safely.

Three **specific, valid** examples of why texting while driving is dangerous are provided as support.

Worse, dealing with text messages requires looking at the device. Even skilled texters take a fast glance before sending a message to make sure it says what was intended. Reading an incoming message requires even more concentration. Every second spent looking at the screen of a phone is time spent NOT looking at the road, in the side-view or rear-view mirror, at the cars driving alongside them or toward them, at pedestrians walking along or waiting to cross, and so on. No matter how good they feel their reflexes are, these drivers can't avoid what they don't see when they are attending to a message instead of looking out the windshield. But worst of all, texting while driving is simply a huge and dangerous distraction. As an August 24, 2009, *Time* article explains,

The supporting examples are arranged in **emphatic order,** signaled by the transitional expressions *For one thing, Worse,* and *Worst of all.*

Note the in-text documentation in accordance with MLA guidelines.

13

although many of us feel that we can multi-task with ease, research indicates that only a small percentage truly can. That means that when the vast majority of drivers are concentrating on sending and receiving text messages, they are not focusing on the road in front of them. In fact, some experts suggest that text messaging while driving is as bad as driving drunk (Cruz and Oloffson). **All in all, the evidence shows that no matter how convenient a means of communication it can be, texting while driving should not be allowed.**

The **closing sentence** restates the significance expressed in the main point and the supporting examples: that texting while driving is a dangerous practice.

A **Work Cited notation** for the article used as support in the writing is included, in keeping with MLA guidelines.

Work Cited

Cruz, Gilbert, and Kristi Oloffson. "Distracted Driving: Should Talking, Texting Be Banned?" *Time Magazine*. Time Online, 24 Aug. 2009. Web. 26 Sept. 2010.

PUTTING ARGUMENT TO WORK

Choose one of the following topics and develop an argument writing of about 100–150 words. Use the annotated writing as a model.

A. Do you think that all drivers—or any group of drivers—should face a road test every five years in order to renew their licenses? Using the model argument above as a guide, take a stand on this issue and provide plenty of support for it.

B. Today's city streets, highways, overpasses, and bridges need regular—and expensive—maintenance. Every level of government seems to find paying for this necessary upkeep difficult. Should all car owners have to pay an annual fee in addition to registration and insurance—perhaps $50 or $100—to be used exclusively for road repair? Decide which side of this issue you are on, and then develop an argument writing like the one on driving while texting to express your viewpoint.

13

FOR ADDITIONAL CONSIDERATION

1. After considering the following topics, prewrite on the one with which you most strongly agree or disagree:
   - Strict dress codes should be imposed and enforced in public high schools.
   - The United States should require all citizens to carry national identification cards.
   - Parents or guardians should never be allowed to coach their own children on any youth league sports teams.
2. Create a draft of about 100–150 words in which you support your stance on the subject you have chosen.
3. Using the Argument Checklist (page 114) as a guide, revise your draft. Make sure that your stance on the subject is explicitly stated and that you have provided sufficient valid support for your point of view, with an appropriate combination of modes and plenty of transition to guide your reader. If you have included expert opinion, check that you have correctly documented its use. At the same time, evaluate the logic, tone, and arrangement to ensure that your point of view comes across clearly and effectively to your reader. Have an objective reader evaluate your draft in terms of these points as well.
4. Addressing any problems you and your reader have identified, create a final draft.

PART III

Issues of Mechanics and Usage

14

Parts of Speech

Understanding the Ways Words Function

To enjoy a full understanding of anything, you first need a working knowledge of the language that describes its essential elements. For writers, this guideline means understanding the names and functions of the eight *parts of speech.*

- the **noun**
- the **pronoun**
- the **adjective**
- the **adverb**
- the **conjunction**
- the **preposition**
- the **interjection**
- the **verb**

Six of the parts of speech can be grouped on the basis of common *functions:* the *namers,* nouns and pronouns; the *modifiers,* adjectives and adverbs; and the *connectors,* conjunctions and prepositions. Interjections and verbs have highly specialized functions, with verbs in particular serving

14

a central role in every sentence you write. A mastery of this information will prepare you to discuss and address aspects of writing related to grammar and usage. It's the foundation you need to write sentences that are simple, clear, and correct.

The Namers—Nouns and Pronouns

Nouns name persons, places, things, and ideas, and pronouns are used in place of nouns and other pronouns. If a word names something that exists in fact or fiction, even if it can't be held, touched, or pointed out, the word is either a noun or a pronoun.

> **Officials** throughout **Indiana, Wisconsin,** and **Nebraska** have faced **frustration** because of the ongoing **floods.**

Here, nouns name persons, *Officials;* places, *Indiana, Wisconsin,* and *Nebraska;* things, *floods;* and an idea, *frustration.*

Proper nouns begin with a capital letter and name specific persons (*Julia*), places (*China*), things (*Civic Engagement*), and ideas (*Utopia*). **Common** nouns name the rest (*woman, country, approach,* and *happiness*).

Nouns serve in six capacities in a sentence: subject, predicate nominative, direct object, indirect object, object of a preposition, and appositive.

- a **subject:**

EXAMPLE: **Management** remains a popular major for many college students.

- a **predicate nominative,** the word that answers "Who or What?" after a linking verb:

EXAMPLE: My cousin is an outstanding **singer.**

- a **direct object,** the word that answers "Whom or What?" after an action verb:

EXAMPLE: Kate opened the **package** on the table.

- an **indirect object,** the word that answers "To Whom or For Whom?" or "To What or For What?" after an action verb:

EXAMPLE: The coach gave the **team** a pep talk.

- an **object of a preposition,** the word that follows a preposition and completes a prepositional phrase:

14

EXAMPLE: The DVD on the **counter** belongs to my cousin.

• an **appositive,** a word that helps to explain or illustrate another noun:

EXAMPLE: The shouts came from the first four rows, the **section** set aside for visiting fans.

Pronouns, like nouns, refer to people, places, things, and ideas, and they can fulfill the same six functions in a sentence as nouns. Pronouns act as a kind of shorthand, allowing you to express your meaning without needless repetition.

Look at the pronouns in this sentence:

EXAMPLE: *Jackie* inserted the *key* into the ignition, but **it** wouldn't turn, and **anybody who** might have given **her** a ride had already left.

Here, the personal pronoun **it** takes the place of the common noun *key,* and the indefinite pronoun **anybody** takes the place of the names of a number of people who otherwise would have to be identified. In addition, the relative pronoun **who** refers to **anybody**, and the personal pronoun **her** takes the place of the proper noun *Jackie.* Chapter 22 covers the use of pronouns in full detail.

The Modifiers—Adjectives and Adverbs

Adjectives and adverbs describe or *modify* other words, so they are known as modifiers. Adjectives modify nouns (and very occasionally pronouns), and adverbs modify verbs, adjectives, and other adverbs.

Adjectives generally answer the questions "Which one?", "How many?", and "What kind?" about the words they are modifying, thus providing a more precise representation for the reader. A noun like *table,* by itself, doesn't create a clear, specific picture. Add some adjectives, however—a dull, scratched, teak *table*—and the image is clearer and more complete.

The most common adjectives are the three known as **articles:** *a, an,* and *the. A* and *an* are called **indefinite articles** because you use them to modify an unspecified noun: *a* for words beginning with a consonant sound (*a* ranch) and *an* for words beginning with a vowel sound (*an* incident). *The* is called a **definite article** because you use it to modify a specific noun: *the* ranch, *the* incident.

Adverbs modify verbs, adjectives, and adverbs and answer the questions "When?", "Where?," "How?", "Why?", and "How much?"

or "To what extent?" They describe how someone or something acts, for example, The children waved *enthusiastically,* or when something occurs, for instance, *Tomorrow,* I will begin studying for my exam. Adverbs also illustrate degree relative to other modifiers, for example, The children waved *very* enthusiastically or The exam was *incredibly* easy.

Many adverbs end in *-ly,* and turning some adjectives into adverbs is a simple matter of adding *-ly:* quick, quick*ly.* But an *-ly* ending doesn't automatically indicate that a word is an adverb. Instead, it depends how the word is being used. *Early* is an adjective when it modifies a noun, for instance, the *early* train, but it's an adverb when it describes when something happened, for example, I went to work *early.* Chapter 23 focuses on the proper use of adjectives and adverbs.

The Connectors—Conjunctions and Prepositions

Conjunctions and prepositions enable you to connect ideas. A conjunction links two or more units of the same type—two or more of the same kind of word, two or more phrases, or two or more clauses (**subject–verb units**). A preposition joins the noun or pronoun following it to some other word in the sentence.

There are three types of conjunctions—*coordinating, correlative,* and *subordinating*—each of which creates a slightly different kind of connection:

COORDINATING CONJUNCTIONS

and	nor	so
but	or	yet
for (because)		

CORRELATIVE CONJUNCTIONS

both/and	neither/nor	whether/or
either/or	not only/but also	

SUBORDINATING CONJUNCTIONS

after	even though	than	whenever
although	if	though	where
as	in order that	unless	wherever
as if	rather than	until	whether
because	since	when	while
before	so that		

14

Note how the conjunctions join the elements within the following sentences:

verb   *verb*

EXAMPLES: The contestants *danced* **and** *sang* all morning.

phrase   *phrase*   *phrase*

In the park, **at the beach,** *or by the pool, parents have to keep a close watch on their children.*

clause

We had to stand during the whole trip **because**

clause

all the seats in the subway car were taken.

With conjunctions, the units you connect must be of the same category. The exception concerns nouns and pronouns because you can link a noun and a pronoun:

noun   *pronoun*

EXAMPLE: *Carmen* **and** *somebody* from work went shopping.

A preposition provides a different kind of connection. The noun or pronoun that follows a preposition is called the object of the preposition, and the resulting unit is called a **prepositional phrase**. In that structure, the preposition links the object of the preposition to some other word in the sentence.

Here is a list of commonly used prepositions, plus a list of common compound prepositions:

PREPOSITIONS

about	at	but (except)	inside	outside	toward
above	before	by	into	over	under
across	behind	despite	like	past	underneath
after	below	down	near	since	unlike
against	beneath	during	of	than	until
along	beside	except	off	through	up
among	besides	for	on	throughout	upon
around	between	from	onto	till	with
as	beyond	in	out	to	within
					without

COMPOUND PREPOSITIONS

according to	because of	in the place of
along with	in addition to	instead of
as to	in front of	next to
aside from	in spite of	out of

When the prepositional phrase modifies a noun, the prepositional phrase functions as an adjective:

EXAMPLE: The *dog* **in the big apartment house** is dangerous.

But when the prepositional phrase modifies a verb, adjective, or adverb, the prepositional phrase functions as an adverb:

EXAMPLES: The dangerous dog *lived* **in the big apartment house.**

Its coat was *black* **with red highlights.**

Its barking and snarling would finally end *early* **in the evening.**

Interjections

Words like *hey, wow, oh, well, ah,* and so on, are interjections, which convey excitement or emotion but have no other real connection to a sentence. If the excitement or emotion is particularly strong, an interjection is followed by an exclamation point. As a writer, however, you should use interjections sparingly, only when there is genuine excitement or emotion in your discussion.

Verbs

Verbs show action or otherwise help to make a statement; for this reason, they may rank as the most important of all the parts of speech. They animate thoughts or add vital meaning in terms of intent, presence, or condition.

Most verbs in English are **action verbs,** words that show action, whether that action is physical or mental, real or imagined—for example, *examine, laugh, think, speak, eat, worry,* and so on.

EXAMPLE: The first officers at an accident scene **control** traffic.

Other verbs, called **linking verbs,** indicate a relationship or link between the main idea and some word in the sentence. Most linking verbs are forms of *to be,* for example, *is, are, was, were, might be, could have been, was being,* and so on. Verbs like *appear, become, feel, grow, look, remain, smell, seem,* and *taste* can serve as linking verbs if they are used to indicate a relationship rather than an action:

14

EXAMPLES: My aunt **is** a nurse practitioner.

Jeremy **seems** so much more confident. (means Jeremy *is* confident)

Helping or **auxiliary verbs** are forms of *be, do,* and *have* (*will be* running, *did* play, *has* traveled) that are used with different tenses of other verbs to form additional tenses that express times and conditions in the past, present, and future. The **modals** *may, might, must, can, should,* and *could* also serve as helping verbs. Chapter 21 covers correct verb use in full detail.

15

Sentence Elements

Considering the Principal Parts

The most basic structure of writing is the **sentence.** This arrangement of language, beginning with a capital letter and ending with a mark of terminal punctuation, communicates a particular meaning to a reader. For a group of words to qualify as a sentence, it needs two primary elements:

- a **verb,** a word that shows action or otherwise helps to make a statement
- a **subject,** the person, place, thing, or idea performing the action or serving as the focus of the discussion

Sentences often contain a third element that completes the action or discussion:

- a **complement**

In addition, writers often use other groups of words to clarify the meaning of the information in a sentence, including:

- phrases
- clauses

15 Each time you set off a group of words as a sentence, you need to evaluate it carefully. That way, you will be sure that it features the primary elements required for a correct sentence and that the resulting unit is simple, clear, and correct.

Subjects and Verbs

In a sentence, the word that shows action or otherwise helps to make a statement is the *verb*. The word that answers the question "Who or what is doing the action or being discussed?" is the *subject*.

EXAMPLES: All of a sudden, the painting fell to the floor.

My younger sister is the best swimmer on her high school team.

In the first sentence, the verb is *fell*. Ask "Who or what fell to the floor?", and the answer, and therefore the subject, is *painting*. In the second sentence, the verb is *is*. The answer to the question "Who or what is the best swimmer on her high school team?"—the subject—is *sister*.

With sentences in the **imperative mood**—often called **direct address** or the **command**—the subject doesn't actually appear in the sentence. Instead, it is implied or *understood* to be the person being addressed, as this example shows:

EXAMPLE: Send a text message to confirm our dinner reservation.

The verb is *send*. Ask the question "Who or what *send a text message to confirm our dinner reservations*?", and the answer, even though the word isn't actually in the sentence, is the person being told to send the text message, the understood subject **You:**

      subject   verb

EXAMPLE: **(You)** Send a text message to confirm our dinner reservation.

Complements

In addition to a subject and a verb, some sentences have a **complement,** a word that completes the action or statement presented in the subject–verb unit. An action verb transfers action directly, so the complement that follows an action verb is called a *direct object*. It is the word that answers the question "Whom or what?" *after* the verb. Take a look at this example:

        subject verb
EXAMPLE: The **punter** *kicked* the ball over 80 yards.

Ask the question "The punter kicked whom or what?", and the answer, *ball,* is the direct object.

    Sometimes sentences containing an action verb and a direct object will have an additional complement. Called an **indirect object,** this type of complement appears between the verb and the direct object and answers the question "To whom, to what, for whom, for what?"

        subject verb   direct object
EXAMPLE: On her way to work, **Kara** *mailed* Trey a **letter.**

Letter receives the action of the verb directly, so it's the direct object. Now ask the question "Kara mailed a letter to whom or to what, for whom or for what?", and the word that answers the question—the word that receives the action indirectly—is *Trey.* It is therefore the indirect object.

    If the verb in a sentence is a linking verb, the complement will be either a **predicate nominative** or a **predicate adjective.** A predicate nominative is a noun or pronoun that answers the question "Who or what?" after a linking verb.

      subject   linking verb predicate nominative
EXAMPLE: My **coworker** for the night *was* my **neighbor.**

Ask the question "My coworker for the night was who or what?", and the answer—the predicate nominative—is **neighbor.**

    As the name suggests, a predicate adjective is an adjective that answers the question "Who or what?" after a linking verb.

          linking predicate
    subject verb adjective
EXAMPLE: **Billy** *can be* very **sarcastic.**

The word that answers the question "Billy can be very who or what?" is the adjective **sarcastic,** which makes it a predicate adjective.

Phrases

A **phrase** is a group of words functioning as a single word. Types of phrases are the following:

- the **verb phrase**—a main verb and an auxiliary verb:

15

EXAMPLE: You **should have** *asked* for assistance sooner.

The auxiliary verb **should have** is combined with *asked* to create a verb phrase.

- the **prepositional phrase**—a preposition, a noun or pronoun serving as its object, and any of its modifiers:

EXAMPLES: The supplies **in that cupboard** are brand new.

At one o'clock, several departments closed **for safety inspection.**

In the first example, **in that cupboard** serves as an adjective modifying *supplies*. In the second example, **At one o'clock** and **for safety inspection** serve as adverbs modifying the verb *closed*. See Chapter 23 for more on modifiers and Chapter 25 for more on prepositional phrases.

- the **verbal phrase**—a *verbal* (a form of a verb that acts as another part of speech) plus any modifiers. There are three types of verbals: **participles, gerunds,** and **infinitives.**

  Participles act as adjectives. Present participles end in *-ing,* and past participles end in *-ed* or *-d* for regular verbs:

  participial phrase
EXAMPLES: **Opening the door wide,** the teacher welcomed the new kindergarten students.

  participial phrase
  Shoved out of bounds, the center immediately gestured to the official.

In the first sentence, the present participial phrase **Opening the door wide** modifies *teacher,* and in the second, the past participial phrase **Shoved out of bounds** modifies *center.*

  Gerunds, which also end in *-ing,* act as nouns:

  gerund phrase
EXAMPLE: **Identifying the exits** in public buildings is an important safety concern.

Here, the gerund phrase **Identifying the exits** answers the question "Who or what is one of the first things to do?", so it serves as the subject of the sentence.

  Infinitives consist of the basic form of a verb preceded by *to* and can act as adjectives, adverbs, or nouns:

  infinitive phrase
EXAMPLE: Edward needed a simple *explanation* **to understand the complex problem.**

15

The infinitive phrase **to understand the complex problem** is acting as an adjective modifying the noun *explanation*.

infinitive phrase
EXAMPLE: The woman *rushed* onto the field **to check on her injured son.**

The infinitive phrase **to check on her injured son** is acting as an adverb modifying the verb *rushed*.

infinitive phrase
EXAMPLE: My brother John plans **to resume all activities soon.**

The infinitive phrase **to resume all activities soon** is acting as a noun. It answers the question "John plans whom or what?", making it the direct object.

Clauses

A clause is a group of words containing a subject–verb unit that functions as a single word. There are two main types of clauses:

- An independent or **main** clause, which makes independent sense
- A dependent or **subordinate** clause, which relies on a main clause to communicate a full meaning

Consider this example, which contains both types of clauses:

EXAMPLE: **Irina finally walked home** *after she had waited an hour for a repair truck.*

The unit **Irina finally walked home** is the main clause because it can stand alone. The second unit, *after she had waited an hour for a repair truck,* doesn't make independent sense, so it is a subordinate clause.

Subordinate clauses act as three parts of speech:

adjective

adjective clause
EXAMPLE: The tablet computer **that Madison bought last week** stopped working today.

The subordinate clause **that Madison bought last week** is acting as an adjective modifying the noun *computer*. (Subordinate clauses like this one, introduced by a relative pronoun like *that, who,* or *which,* are also called **relative clauses.**)

15

adverb

adverb clause

EXAMPLE: **When I called my date the wrong name,** the night was ruined.

The subordinate clause **When I called my date the wrong name** is acting as an adverb modifying the verb phrase *was ruined*.

noun

noun clause

EXAMPLE: **What the researchers predicted** was widespread contamination from the oil spill.

The subordinate clause **What the researchers predicted** answers the question "Who or what was widespread contamination from the oil spill?", so it is acting as a noun serving as the subject of the verb *was*.

16

The Types of Sentences

Understanding the Different Methods

Interpersonal communication is complicated and multifaceted. Sometimes we make statements, sometimes we make inquiries, sometimes we direct others, and sometimes we express great excitement or emotion. As a writer, you will create four different types of sentences that serve these purposes and capture or express those specific kinds of interactions:

- the declarative sentence
- the interrogative sentence
- the imperative sentence
- the exclamatory sentence

Once you understand the differences among these sentence types, you will be that much more likely to write exactly the type of sentence appropriate to convey your intent. At the same time, you will help ensure that your writing remains simple, clear, and correct.

16

The Declarative Sentence

A sentence that makes a statement is called a *declarative sentence:*

EXAMPLE: My new phone has an amazing number of special features.

The Interrogative Sentence

A sentence that asks a direct question is known as an *interrogative sentence:*

EXAMPLE: When does my new phone contract begin?

A sentence that asks an indirect question is actually a declarative sentence, which calls for a period, not a question mark, at the end:

Indirect Declarative Sentence: The customer service representative asked which apps to include.

The Imperative Sentence

A sentence that expresses a command or request is called an *imperative sentence.* The subject of an imperative sentence, called *you understood,* is implied or understood to be the person who is receiving the command:

EXAMPLES: Charge your phone at least every other day.

(You) Charge your phone at least every other day.

The Exclamatory Sentence

A sentence that expresses strong excitement or emotion is known as an *exclamatory sentence,* and this type of sentence always ends in an exclamation point:

EXAMPLE: That phone may be the best birthday present ever!

17

The Classifications of Sentences

Considering Different Structures

As Chapter 15, "Sentence Elements," makes clear, a group of words is a complete sentence when it contains a verb plus its subject and expresses a complete thought. But writers often go beyond this basic pattern, combining subject and verb units in different ways. The resulting sentences can be classified in four ways based on the number and characteristics of the subject–verb units called *clauses:*

- simple sentence
- compound sentence
- complex sentence
- compound-complex sentence

These different classes of sentences offer you variety and flexibility regarding how you express your ideas. Your ultimate goal is to choose the approach that most effectively communicates your meaning and keeps your writing simple, clear, and correct.

17

The Simple Sentence

A *simple sentence* consists of a main or independent clause set off by itself:

EXAMPLE: The latest 3D televisions have amazing picture quality.

The Compound Sentence

A *compound sentence* is composed of two or more main clauses connected by a coordinating conjunction or a semicolon:

EXAMPLES: Snow was accumulating rapidly, **and** a fierce wind made the situation even worse.

Snow was accumulating rapidly**;** a fierce wind made the situation even worse.

The Complex Sentence

A *complex sentence* consists of a main clause connected to one or more subordinate clauses:

EXAMPLES: *After the lights came back on,* **people all around the city resumed their normal routines.**

The technician *who installed the alarm system* **returned to take care of the problems this morning.**

The Compound-Complex Sentence

A *compound-complex sentence* is composed of two or more main clauses connected by a coordinating conjunction or a semicolon, plus one or more subordinate clauses:

EXAMPLE: **The restaurant** *that we had chosen* **was jammed,** and *when we were finally called,* **the hostess sat us next to restrooms.**

When it comes to classifications of sentences, always use the combination that best helps you communicate your message to your reader.

PART IV

Common Problem Spots—Identification and Elimination

137

18

Fragments

Distinguishing between Complete and Incomplete Units

You've probably had the experience yourself: you walked into a room, tuned into a conversation, and immediately got the wrong impression. You thought the discussion concerned sports, for example, or online gaming, but it was actually about another subject entirely. How could you have been so far off in terms of what was being discussed? The explanation is that you heard only a portion, a fragment of the conversation, and so you were confused or misled. In writing, a **fragment** is an incomplete sentence, a unit that doesn't communicate its ideas and thus can't stand alone and make independent sense. This error appears in several different forms in writing, including

- missing subject or missing verb fragments
- phrase fragments
- subordinate clause fragments

The key point to keep in mind about fragments is that they are incomplete expressions of your ideas. It is vital to find and eliminate them from your writing. They keep your reader from gaining a full understanding of the point you want to express—and therefore keep your writing from being simple, clear, and correct.

Omitted Subject or Verb Fragments

As Chapter 15 illustrates, a sentence must have a verb and its subject. If either part is missing, the group of words is not a sentence—it's a fragment.

To find any fragments of this type, look first for a verb in the group of words. If there is no verb, you have a fragment:

Faulty: The manager of the gym near my house.

To eliminate the fragment, supply an appropriate verb:

verb
Corrected: The manager of the gym near my house **called.**

If you identify a verb, then look for the subject by asking, "Who or what?" before the verb. If no word answers the question, you have a fragment.

verb
Faulty: *Told* Nick's supervisor about his most recent evaluation.

To eliminate the fragment, supply an appropriate noun or pronoun that answers the question "Who or what told Nick's supervisor about his most recent evaluation?"

subject   *verb*
Corrected: **The district manager** *told* Nick's supervisor about his most recent evaluation.

Correcting Phrase Fragments

As Chapter 15 spells out (pages 129–131), a **phrase** consists of two or more words that function as a single word. Common types of phrases include **verb phrases, prepositional phrases, verbal phrases,** and **appositive phrases.** Because a phrase doesn't contain a subject–verb unit, a phrase set off by itself is always a fragment.

Verb Phrase Fragments Verb phrases, as Chapter 15 (pages 129–130) explains, consist of a main verb plus a helping verb (*is, were, will be,*

18

and so on) or a modal (*may, can, must,* and so on). Because a verb phrase set off by itself lacks a subject, it is a fragment:

Verb Phrase Fragment: Will be cheering.

To correct this type of fragment, simply add a subject, as this version shows:

Corrected: In a few days, a huge crowd of supporters will be cheering.

Prepositional Phrase Fragments   As Chapter 14 (pages 124–125) details, prepositional phrases consist of a preposition and a noun or pronoun that acts as the object of the preposition, plus all the words in between. Here again are the lists of prepositions presented in Chapter 14:

PREPOSITIONS

about	before	despite	near	than	up
above	behind	down	of	through	upon
across	below	during	off	throughout	with
after	beneath	except	on	till	within
against	beside	for	onto	to	without
along	besides	from	out	toward	
among	between	in	outside	under	
around	beyond	inside	over	underneath	
as	but (except)	into	past	unlike	
at	by	like	since	until	

COMPOUND PREPOSITIONS

according to	because of	in the place of
along with	in addition to	instead of
as to	in front of	next to
aside from	in spite of	out of

Set off by itself, a prepositional phrase is a fragment because it lacks a subject–verb unit:

Prepositional Phrase Fragment: Under his grandmother's old refrigerator.

Often the solution to this kind of fragment is simple: combine the phrase with the preceding or following sentence to which the phrase fragment logically belongs:

Corrected: *Under his grandmother's old refrigerator,* **Zak found her missing birth certificate.**

Other times, you will need to generate a subject–verb unit and other words and then add them to the prepositional phrase to create a complete sentence:

Corrected: **Over the years, a number of documents had slipped** *under his grandmother's old refrigerator.*

Verbal Phrase Fragments A verbal phrase consists of a verbal plus any words accompanying it. As Chapter 15 explains, verbals, which include *participles, gerunds,* and *infinitives,* are verb forms that act as other parts of speech. Present participles end in *-ing* and act as adjectives, and gerunds end in *-ing* and act as nouns. Infinitives are simple present tense forms of a verb introduced by *to,* and they act as adjectives, adverbs, or nouns.

Even though a verbal is a verb form, it can't serve as the verb in a sentence. But because it resembles a verb, you might think that you have written a sentence when you actually have written a fragment. Take a look at these examples:

sentence

Faulty: Many people have begun signing up for yoga classes at the
infinitive phrase fragment
community center. *To deal with stress in their lives.*

sentence

Faulty: Once the semester is over, I will investigate ways to get
participial phrase fragment
some on-the-job experience. *Including possible internships.*

In both passages, the initial unit is a complete sentence because it can make independent sense. But the second unit can't make independent sense because the verbal phrase lacks a subject–verb unit.

To correct a verbal phrase fragment, you can add it before or after the sentence to which it logically belongs:

Corrected: Many people have begun signing up for yoga classes at the community center *to deal with stress in their lives.*

18

You can also rephrase the fragment and include a subject–verb unit to create a complete sentence:

Corrected: **Once the semester is over, I will investigate ways to get some on-the-job experience.** *The possibilities include internships.*

Appositive Phrase Fragments An individual word or group of words explaining or renaming a noun or pronoun that precedes it is known as an *appositive*. Some appositives are long and may seem to be sentences, but they're not because they can't stand on their own.

Look at this example:

sentence

Faulty: **Tim hates to reconcile his credit card account.**

appositive fragment

A boring and frustrating task.

The first group of words is a sentence because it makes sense by itself. But the second group, *A boring and frustrating task,* can't stand on its own because it lacks a verb.

Appositives generally follow the word they explain or rename, so you can easily eliminate an appositive fragment by adding it to the sentence that contains the word the appositive explains or renames:

Corrected: **Tim hates to reconcile his credit card account,** *a boring and frustrating task.*

Correcting Subordinate Clause Fragments

Probably the most common fragments result from dependent or **subordinate clauses** being set off as sentences. Unlike phrases, subordinate clauses *do* contain subjects and verbs, which explains why writers so often set them off as sentences. But as Chapter 15 (pages 131–132) explains, subordinate clauses are fragments because they can't communicate their messages independently. Instead, they depend upon main clauses to express their full meanings.

18

SUBORDINATING CONJUNCTIONS

after	even though	than	whenever
although	if	though	where
as	in order that	unless	wherever
as if	rather than	until	whether
because	since	when	while
before	so that		

Subordinate clause fragments are often introduced by one of the following subordinating conjunctions:

subordinate clause fragment

Faulty: *After the heavy rain had subsided and the wind had finally*

sentence

died down. **The streets were filled with leaves, small branches, and other debris.**

To eliminate subordinate clause fragments introduced by subordinating conjunctions, you can combine the subordinate clause with the main clause to which it logically belongs:

Corrected: *After the heavy rain had subsided and the wind had finally. died down,* **the streets were filled with leaves, small branches, and other debris.**

You can also remove the conjunction and create two sentences:

Corrected: *The heavy rain had subsided and the wind had finally died down.* **The streets were filled with leaves, small branches, and other debris.**

The following *relative pronouns* introduce another type of subordinate clause—the **relative clause:**

RELATIVE PRONOUNS

who	whom	which
	whose	that

18

When it is set off by itself, a relative clause is a fragment:

sentence

Faulty: My brother had filled the box with bubble wrap and

relative clause fragment

other packing material. *Which kept the small figurine from breaking.*

To eliminate this kind of fragment, simply combine the two clauses:

Corrected: My brother had filled the box with bubble wrap and other packing material, *which kept the small figurine from breaking.*

Who, whom, which, and *whose* can be used to introduce sentences that ask questions. In these cases, the pronouns are called *interrogative pronouns* and the units are not fragments but **interrogative sentences:**

EXAMPLES: Which tablet computer would be best for the average college student?

Who signed for the package?

The key to knowing whether a group of words introduced by *who, whom, which,* or *whose* is a sentence or a fragment is the punctuation mark at the end. If there is a question mark, the unit is likely a sentence. But if no question mark follows the unit, you most likely have a relative pronoun introducing a subordinate clause fragment.

19

Comma Splices and Run-on Sentences

Correctly Connecting or Separating Your Ideas

When it comes to the sentences you write, you have two main choices: you can connect them or you can separate them. What you *can't* do, however, is simply put one after the other, with nothing connecting or separating them. Your reader counts on you to show where one idea ends and the next begins. When you fail to indicate this point, the result is one of two common—and serious—sentence errors, the **comma splice** or the **run-on sentence**. A comma splice involves using a comma to connect two sentences. The problem is that *commas can't connect*. A run-on sentence, sometimes called a *fused sentence,* results when two or more sentences don't have a proper connector or separator. To keep your writing free from comma splices and run-on sentences, you need to concentrate on a number of techniques, including

- using conjunctions to connect sentences
- using semicolons to connect sentences
- using end punctuation to separate sentences

19

Comma splices and run-on sentences are significant concerns. They suggest to your reader that you don't know where one idea ends and the next idea begins. As a result, these sentence errors keep your writing from being simple, clear, and correct.

The Key to Finding Comma Splices and Run-on Sentences

To find comma splices and run-on sentences in your writing, first identify all subjects and verbs in the units that you set off as independent ideas. Then, for any sentences containing more than one subject–verb unit, make sure that these units are properly connected. Take a look at the following examples:

> subject   verb   subject
> **Comma Splice:** The *party* **started** at 8 p.m, / *Shaniqua* finally
> verb
> **arrived** at 9:30.

> subject   verb
> **Run-on Sentence:** A *number* of sites **offer** television viewing on
> subject verb
> demand / *HULU* **is** one of the more popular options.

In the first example, a comma comes between the subject–verb units (separated by a slash), each of which could stand as a simple sentence by itself. But *commas can't connect*, so the result is a comma splice. In the second example, the first subject–verb unit *runs into* the second, with no connector or separator between them. The result is a run-on sentence.

A Conjunction to Connect Sentences

One method to eliminate comma splices and run-on sentences is to connect the two sentences with one of three kinds of conjunctions: **coordinating conjunctions, correlative conjunctions,** and **subordinating conjunctions.**

Coordinating conjunctions (*and, or, but,* and so on) indicate basic relationships between the elements being connected. *And* acts like the plus sign (+) in mathematics, while *or* indicates an alternative and *but* suggests an exception.

Correlative conjunctions (*neither/nor, not only/but also, both/and,* and so on) are pairs of conjunctions that specify relationships between two units. *Either/or* points to only one of two possibilities, whereas *not only/ but also* stresses both elements, as does *both/and.*

Subordinating conjunctions (*because, if, when,* and so on) also express a conditional relationship between clauses. *Although* indicates an exception or deviation from an expectation, *if* suggests a possibility or contingency, and *when* emphasizes time relative to something else. See page 123 for complete lists of the three types of conjunctions.

To correct a comma splice using a conjunction, place the conjunction immediately following the comma between the clauses:

Comma Splice: The exterior of the car was badly dented, / the interior was in even worse shape.

Corrected: The exterior of the car was badly dented, **but** the interior was in even worse shape.

The coordinating conjunction **but** now connects the two clauses, indicating a contrary relationship between them.

To correct a run-on sentence with a conjunction, place the conjunction between the two subject–verb units:

Run-on Sentence: Tresley devotes most of his spare time to training for triathlons / he still manages to volunteer at the Boys and Girls Club.

Corrected: Tresley devotes most of his spare time to training for triathlons / **although** he still manages to volunteer at the Boys and Girls Club.

Here the subordinating conjunction **although** connects the two clauses, emphasizing a contrary or conditional relationship between them.

When a subordinate clause like *although* appears in the second unit of a sentence, you don't need a comma before the conjunction. If you reverse the order of the clauses, however, put a comma between them to provide the needed pause.

Corrected: **Although** he still manages to volunteer at the Boys and Girls Club, Tresley devotes most of his spare time to training for triathlons.

A Semicolon to Connect Sentences

Another way to correct a comma splice or run-on sentence is to put a semicolon between the clauses. A semicolon has roughly the same meaning as a comma plus *and*, but it suggests that the two clauses are so closely linked in meaning or message that no additional word is necessary to show their connection.

Take a look at this example:

Comma Splice: The Civic Center is a terrible place for a concert, / the lighting and sound system are both inadequate.

Here, the first subject–verb unit sets up the reader's expectations by stating that the nightclub was in poor shape, and the second unit follows through by giving examples of what was wrong with the place. For this reason, a semicolon in place of the comma would be a good choice to correct the comma splice:

Corrected: The Civic Center is a terrible place for a concert; the lighting and sound system are both inadequate.

Now consider this example:

Run-on Sentence: All I wanted was to take a shower and enjoy a quiet meal / things just didn't work out that way.

Here, the first clause tells the reader what the plans were, and the second indicates a departure from those plans, so a semicolon between the subject–verb units would be a good choice to eliminate the run-on sentence:

Corrected: All I wanted was to take a shower and enjoy a quiet meal; things just didn't work out that way.

To suggest an additional relationship, include one of the following **conjunctive adverbs** immediately after the semicolon:

19

CONJUNCTIVE ADVERBS

also	however	similarly
besides	instead	still
consequently	meanwhile	then
finally	moreover	therefore
furthermore	nevertheless	thus

Always keep in mind that conjunctive adverbs are *adverbs*, not conjunctions, so they have no power to connect. Therefore, when you add a conjunctive adverb between clauses, you must use a semicolon to provide the necessary connection and a comma after the conjunctive adverb:

Corrected: All I wanted was to take a shower and enjoy a quiet meal; **however,** things just didn't work out that way.

End Punctuation to Create Separate Sentences

A third method that eliminates comma splices and run-on sentences does so by turning the subject–verb units into individual sentences. This approach involves putting a period or other appropriate mark of terminal punctuation between the independent clauses. From the standpoint of style, this option is a good choice when the subject–verb units are fairly long.

Consider this example:

Comma Splice: The flight from Phoenix to O'Hare Airport in Chicago, which is among the busiest airports in the country, was unsettling because of turbulence, / the flight to Orlando, with several groups of excited high school kids on their way to enjoy the different theme parks, was almost as bad.

The first clause by itself is 23 words long, so it makes sense to eliminate the comma splice by changing the comma between the subject–verb units to a period and then capitalizing the first word of the second clause:

19

Corrected: The flight from Phoenix to O'Hare Airport in Chicago, which is among the busiest airports in the country, was unsettling because of turbulence. The flight to Orlando, with several groups of excited high school kids on their way to enjoy the different theme parks, was almost as bad.

To use a period to correct a run-on sentence, first find the point at which the first clause ends and the second clause begins:

Run-on Sentence: Lauren's new computer, which cost almost $1,500, including the software, is such an improvement over her last one / now she is able to do all her work much more quickly, and the computer doesn't freeze up when she is playing computer games or spending time on her Facebook page.

Then put a period (or, if appropriate, a question mark or exclamation point) at the end of the first subject–verb unit and capitalize the first word of the second unit:

Corrected: Lauren's new computer, which cost almost $1,500, including the software, is such an improvement over her last one. **Now** she is able to do all her work much more quickly, and the computer doesn't freeze up when she is playing computer games or spending time on her Facebook page.

Using a period to eliminate a comma splice or run-on sentence makes sense when the independent units are fairly long, as they are with these examples. But a period would be a bad choice with short independent clauses because it would make your writing choppy, as this example shows:

Choppy: The player launched a desperation shot from the half court line. The shot hit the back of the rim and bounced out of bounds.

A better choice with relatively short sentences like these would be to connect the clauses with a conjunction or a semicolon, with or without a conjunctive adverb:

19

Improved: The player launched a desperation shot from the half court line, **but** the shot hit the back of the rim and bounced out of bounds.

Improved: The player launched a desperation shot from the half court line; **the** shot hit the back of the rim and bounced out of bounds.

Improved: The player launched a desperation shot from the half court line; **however,** the shot hit the back of the rim and bounced out of bounds.

Using any of these methods to combine these brief subject–verb units makes the writing flow more smoothly than would setting the units off as separate sentences.

20

Subject–Verb Agreement

Matching Up the Key Parts

In business, an agreement is a document that outlines the role each party will play in a joint enterprise, ensuring that things go smoothly in that relationship. In the sentences you write, *agreement* also refers to a relationship between parties, in this case, between subjects and verbs. For a sentence to be correct, these two parts must agree or match up in terms of number—*singular,* referring to one, or *plural,* referring to more than one. Singular subjects call for singular verb forms, and plural subjects call for plural verb forms. Certain constructions can make it more difficult to maintain subject–verb agreement, including sentences in which

- the subject follows the verb
- phrases or clauses come between subject and verb
- the subject is compound
- the subject is an indefinite pronoun, a collective noun, a singular noun ending in *-s,* or a noun of measurement, amount, or distance

Correct subject–verb agreement helps to keep your reader's attention on your good ideas. Therefore, learning how to identify and eliminate errors in subject–verb agreement will help keep your sentences simple, clear, and correct.

When the Subject Follows the Verb

In the majority of the sentences you write, the subject will come before the verb. In some cases, though, the subject follows the verb or part of the verb, as with a question, for example:

verb   subject   verb

EXAMPLE: *Did* **Michelle** actually *refuse* the promotion?

For the most part, correct subject–verb agreement with questions is easy to maintain. However, one common error occurs when the plural form *don't* comes before a singular subject:

Faulty: *Don't* **Jimmy** *understand* the installation process?

To eliminate this faulty subject–verb agreement, use the verb form that matches the singular subject **Jimmy:**

Corrected: *Doesn't* **Jimmy** *understand* the installation process?

Sentences beginning with *there* or *here* also often present problems. *There* and *here* are adverbs, which can't serve as the subject of a sentence. Whenever a sentence begins with either of these words, the subject comes *after* the verb.

Faulty: There *is* several alternative **routes** to avoid the highway reconstruction.

Here *come* my **friend.**

In the first sentence, the verb is the singular *is*. When you ask the question "Who or what *is* there for her bizarre behavior?", the answer—the subject—is the plural noun **reasons,** so the singular verb *is* is an error in subject–verb agreement. In the second sentence, the verb is the plural *come*. The word that answers the question "Who or what *come* here?" is the singular noun **friend,** again a mistake in subject–verb agreement.

To eliminate these kinds of errors in subject–verb agreement, simply change the subject or the verb so that they agree:

Corrected: There *are* several **routes** available to avoid the highway reconstruction.

or

There *is* **one primary route** available to avoid the highway reconstruction.

20

Corrected: Here *come* my **friends.**

or

Here *comes* my **friend.**

Even better from a stylistic standpoint, restate the sentence to eliminate *there* or *here:*

Corrected: Several **routes** are available to avoid the highway reconstruction.

My **friends** are coming.

When Phrases or Clauses Come between Subjects and Verbs

The greater the separation between the subject and the verb, the more likely you are to make a mistake in subject–verb agreement. With this kind of error in subject–verb agreement, phrases and clauses are the most common interrupting words.

Subjects and Verbs Separated by Phrases

Errors in subject–verb agreement often occur because phrases come between subjects and verbs. Take a look at the following sentence—which of the two verbs is correct?

EXAMPLE: The box on the floor beside the vacuum cleaner and behind the rolls of paper towels (holds/hold) cleaning supplies.

The words that come between the subject and verb—*on the floor, beside the vacuum cleaner, behind the rolls,* and *of paper towels*—are prepositional phrases. Each of these units consists of a preposition and a noun or pronoun serving as the object of the preposition. (See page 124 for a complete listing of prepositions.)

What complicates things with sentences like this one is that an object of the preposition, *towels,* comes right before the verb. As a result, you might incorrectly select *hold* because it agrees with *towels.* Computerized grammar checkers often suggest this incorrect choice as well. But *towels* isn't the subject of the verb because an *object can't be a subject,* so the object of a prepositional phrase will never be the subject of a sentence.

That several other items are mentioned—floor, vacuum cleaner, rolls, and paper towels—might also lead you to choose the plural verb. But only one item—the *box*—*holds* cleaning supplies.

When compound prepositions like *along with* and *in addition to* introduce phrases that come between the subject and verb, you might also have difficulty identifying the actual subject. (For a complete list of compound prepositions, see page 124.) Which is the correct verb in the following sentence?

EXAMPLE: Dr. Alex Matos, along with Attorney Lyman Gorman and CPA Lauren Thorpe, (rents/rent) office space in the same building.

You might have initially concluded that because three people are mentioned, the verb should be the plural form *rent*. But *along with* is a compound preposition, and *Attorney Lyman Gorman and CPA Lauren Thorpe* are objects of that preposition. An object can't be a subject, so the answer to the question "Who or what rents/rent office space in the same building?"—the actual subject—is the singular proper noun *Dr. Alex Matos*. The correct verb is therefore the singular form *rents*.

Subjects and Verbs Separated by Clauses

Subordinate clauses coming between subjects and verbs can often lead to errors in subject–verb agreement. What is the proper verb in the following sentence?

EXAMPLE: The dance floor, *which extends to those large tables,* (needs/need) to be polished once a week.

First, identify the main clause, the subject–verb unit that makes independent sense. In this case, the clause that can stand on its own is **The dance floor (needs/need) to be polished once a week.** The remaining clause, *which extends to those large tables,* can't make independent sense, so it's the subordinate clause.

Now identify the verb in the main clause. Ask the question "Who or what **needs/need** to be polished once a week?", and the answer—the singular noun **floor**—is the subject. The correct verb is therefore the singular form **needs.**

But if you fail to take the time to identify the actual subject of the main clause, you might mistakenly make the verb of the main clause agree with *tables* rather than with the actual subject, **floor.** Computerized grammar-checking features often offer this incorrect alternative. To avoid these kinds of errors, concentrate on the actual subject and verb and disregard the intervening phrases and clauses.

When a Sentence Has a Compound Subject

Compound subjects—which are made up of more than one noun or pronoun connected by a conjunction—can be singular or plural. The conjunction connecting the words will determine the number.

Subjects connected by *and* are almost always plural, regardless of whether the subjects being connected are singular—for example, A hamster and a cat *are* not compatible—or plural—for example, Hamsters and cats *are* not compatible. The exception concerns subjects that are commonly thought of as singular, such as *bacon and eggs, peace and quiet, ham and beans, rock and roll,* and so on.

Using *or* (or *either/or*) to connect subjects indicates that only one of the alternatives is possible. If both subjects are singular—*Nick or Jack*—the verb must have a singular form: *recognizes.* If both subjects are plural—*charts or maps*—the verb must have a plural form—*illustrate.* Although *neither/nor* indicates an absence of something on the part of both subjects, the rules are the same. If both subjects are singular, the verb must have a singular form—Neither Nick nor Jack *recognizes.* If both subjects are plural—Neither charts nor maps *illustrate*—the verb must have a plural form.

When the compound subject consists of both a singular word and a plural word, the verb agrees with the word closer to it:

EXAMPLE: Either the coach or the **starting players** *deserve* the blame for the unexpected loss.

If you reverse the order of the subjects so that the singular **coach** is closer to the verb, the correct verb is then the singular form, *deserves:*

EXAMPLE: Either the starting players or the **coach** *deserves* the blame for the unexpected loss.

When a Subject Is an Indefinite Pronoun, Collective Noun, Singular Noun Ending in -s, or a Noun of Measurement, Amount, or Distance

As Chapter 22 (pages 181–182) explains, indefinite pronouns refer to general rather than specific persons and things. Some indefinite pronouns like *anybody, everyone, somebody, no one,* and so on, are always singular and require a singular verb:

20

EXAMPLE: **Everyone** in my neighborhood *remembers* last fall's power outage.

Both, few, many, and *several* are always plural:

EXAMPLE: **Many** of those bikes *cost* over $1,000.

And *all, any, more, most, none,* and *some* are either singular or plural, depending on the words to which they refer:

EXAMPLES: **All** of the **milk** *has* been destroyed.

All of the **packages** *have* been delivered.

In the first example, **All** refers to the singular noun **milk,** so the proper verb choice is *has been destroyed.* In the second example, though, **All** refers to the plural noun **packages,** so the proper verb choice is *have been delivered.*

Collective nouns are singular words that name groups of items or individuals—for example, *audience, class, committee, faculty, flock, herd, jury, swarm,* and *team.* Use a singular verb with collective nouns:

EXAMPLES: At every concert, the **audience** *breaks* into cheers as soon as the stage lights come on.

The entire **herd** *congregates* near the small pond.

A number of nouns that end in *-s* are actually singular, including nouns like *economics, ethics, mathematics, measles, mumps, news, physics,* and *politics.* Use a singular form of a verb with these nouns:

EXAMPLES: **Mathematics** sometimes *intimidates* students.

Mumps *involves* serious health risks for the unvaccinated, including potential hearing loss and brain and spinal cord inflammation.

Nouns signifying amounts of measurement, money, time, weight, and so on, are also singular. Use a singular verb form with them:

EXAMPLES: **Fifty pounds** *represents* serious weight loss.

Ten days *seems* like a lifetime to a child waiting for a birthday party.

20

Finally, some words, including *antelope, deer, fish, sheep,* and *trout,* have the same singular and plural form. Your choice of singular or plural verb depends on whether you mean one:

EXAMPLE: That **deer** *ran* right in front of the tractor trailer.

or more than one:

EXAMPLE: Those **deer** standing along the edge of the woods *look* well fed.

21

Correct Verb Use: Regular and Irregular Forms, Tense, and Voice

OVERVIEW

Mastering the Different Aspects of Verb Use

If a sentence were a wagon wheel, then the center of that wheel, the hub from which the rest of the wheel radiates, would be the verb. In many ways, verbs are the most important part of speech to you as a writer. As Chapter 14 explains, verbs show action—*talk, exclaim, run, eat,* and so on—or otherwise help to make a statement—*is, am, was, will be, seem, feel,* and so on. To develop a solid understanding of verb use, you need to concentrate on

- regular and irregular verb forms
- verb tense
- verb voice

This part of speech enables you to indicate time periods, announce or declare points, issue commands, ask questions, and so on. In other words, verbs help you bring your thoughts to life or into action, and mastery of their use will help you keep the sentences you write simple, clear, and correct.

21 | Using Irregular Verbs Correctly

Regular verbs in English form their past and past participles by adding -*ed*:

Present	Past	Past Participle
play	play**ed**	(*has, had, have,* or *will have*) play**ed**

Or, if the verb already ends in -*e*, just add -*d:*

Present	Past	Past Participle
coincide	coincid**ed**	(*has, had, have,* or *will have*) coincid**ed**

But **irregular** verbs form their past and past participles in ways that seem, at the least, arbitrary and unpredictable. Consider the forms of the irregular verbs *fight* and *fly:*

Present	Past	Past Participle
fight	**fought**	(*has, had, have,* or *will have*) **fought**
fly	**flew**	(*has, had, have,* or *will have*) **flown**

The following list provides the principal parts of the most common irregular verbs (except for the present participles, which you always create by adding -*ing* to the present tense form):

IRREGULAR VERBS

Present	Past Tense	Past Participle
am, is, are	was, were	been
arise	arose	arisen
awaken	awoke, awaked	awaked, awoke
become	became	become
begin	began	begun
bend	bent	bent
bind	bound	bound
bite	bit	bitten, bit
bleed	bled	bled
blow	blew	blown

21

Present	Past Tense	Past Participle
break	broke	broken
bring	brought	brought
build	built	built
burn	burned, burnt	burned, burnt
burst	burst	burst
buy	bought	bought
catch	caught	caught
choose	chose	chosen
cling	clung	clung
come	came	come
cost	cost	cost
creep	crept	crept
cut	cut	cut
deal	dealt	dealt
dig	dug	dug
dive	dived, dove	dived
do, does	did	done
draw	drew	drawn
dream	dreamed, dreamt	dreamed, dreamt
drink	drank	drunk
drive	drove	driven
eat	ate	eaten
fall	fell	fallen
feed	fed	fed
feel	felt	felt
fight	fought	fought
find	found	found
flee	fled	fled
fling	flung	flung
fly	flew	flown
forbid	forbade, forbad	forbidden, forbid
forget	forgot	forgotten, forgot

(continued)

21

IRREGULAR VERBS (Continued)

Present	Past Tense	Past Participle
freeze	froze	frozen
get	got	got, gotten
give	gave	given
go, goes	went	gone
grind	ground	ground
grow	grew	grown
hang	hung	hung
hang (execute)	hanged	hanged
have, has	had	had
hear	heard	heard
hide	hid	hidden, hid
hold	held	held
hurt	hurt	hurt
keep	kept	kept
kneel	knelt, kneeled	knelt, kneeled
knit	knitted, knit	knitted, knit
know	knew	known
lay	laid	laid
lead	led	led
leap	leaped, leapt	leaped, leapt
leave	left	left
lend	lent	lent
let	let	let
lie	lay	lain
light	lighted, lit	lighted, lit
lose	lost	lost
make	made	made
mean	meant	meant
meet	met	met
mistake	mistook	mistaken
pay	paid	paid
plead	pleaded, pled	pleaded, pled

Present	Past Tense	Past Participle
prove	proved	proved, proven
put	put	put
quit	quit	quit
raise	raised	raised
read	read	read
ride	rode	ridden
ring	rang	rung
rise	rose	risen
run	ran	run
say	said	said
see	saw	seen
seek	sought	sought
sell	sold	sold
send	sent	sent
set	set	set
sew	sewed	sewn, sewed
shake	shook	shaken
shine	shone, shined	shone, shined
shine (polish)	shined	shined
shoot	shot	shot
show	showed	shown, showed
shrink	shrank, shrunk	shrunk, shrunken
shut	shut	shut
sing	sang, sung	sung
sit	sat	sat
sleep	slept	slept
slide	slid	slid
sling	slung	slung
slink	slunk	slunk
sow	sowed	sown, sowed
speak	spoke	spoken
speed	sped, speeded	sped, speeded

(continued)

21

IRREGULAR VERBS (Continued)

Present	Past Tense	Past Participle
spell	spelled, spelt	spelled, spelt
spend	spent	spent
spit	spit, spat	spit, spat
spring	sprang, sprung	sprung
stand	stood	stood
steal	stole	stolen
stick	stuck	stuck
sting	stung	stung
stink	stank, stunk	stunk
stride	strode	stridden
strike	struck	struck, stricken
string	strung	strung
strive	strived, strove	strived, striven
swear	swore	sworn
sweat	sweat, sweated	sweat, sweated
swell	swelled	swelled, swollen
swim	swam	swum
swing	swung	swung
take	took	taken
teach	taught	taught
tear	tore	torn
tell	told	told
throw	threw	thrown
understand	understood	understood
wake	woke, waked	waked, woken
wear	wore	worn
weave	weaved	weaved
weave (cloth)	wove	woven, wove
weep	wept	wept
win	won	won
wind	wound	wound
wring	wrung	wrung
write	wrote	written

To master the use of irregular verbs, go through this list and highlight those verbs that give you trouble. Pay particular attention to the verbs in the right-hand column, the past participles, which always require a form of *to have*.

Also, isolate and then group verbs that follow certain patterns, for example:

- **the same form for the present tense, past tense, and past participle**

Present	Past	Past Participle (with *has, had, have,* or *will have*)
burst	burst	burst
cut	cut	cut
let	let	let
read	read	read

- **the same form for both the past tense and the past participle**

Present	Past	Past Participle (with *has, had, have,* or *will have*)
bring	brought	brought
feel	felt	felt
mean	meant	meant
teach	taught	taught

- **the same change—*i* to *a* to *u*—as the verbs move from the present to the past tense**

Present	Past	Past Participle (with *has, had, have,* or *will have*)
begin	began	begun
drink	drank	drunk
ring	rang	rung
sing	sang	sung

- **the past participles formed by adding an -*n* to the end of the present tense**

Present	Past	Past Participle (with *has, had, have,* or *will have*)
blow	blew	blown
grow	grew	grown
know	knew	known
throw	threw	thrown

21

Finally, for a particularly troublesome irregular verb, create a series of related sentences in which you correctly use the forms of the verb. This will help you learn to use the correct forms whenever you use them:

EXAMPLES: Most mornings I **drink** two cups of coffee before work. Yesterday, I **drank a third cup at home**. Sometimes, I **have drunk** as many as eight cups by the end of the workday.

He often **wears** jeans and running shoes. Yesterday, he **wore** dress shoes with his jeans. By then, he **had worn** the same jeans for over a week.

Recognizing Different Verb Tenses

With verbs, *tense* means "time." All verbs have several tenses, each of which allows you to express a different period or aspect of time. Take a look at the following examples using the regular verb *talk* and the irregular verb *choose*.

The Simple Tenses

The **simple present tense** of a verb shows in one word something that is happening at that time or that happens habitually. The present tense of a verb ends in *-s* for singular subjects, except *I* and *you:*

EXAMPLES: Nursery school students often **talk** loudly.

Instructors usually **choose** activities to help students better understand the class material.

The **simple past tense** shows in one word what has already occurred. With regular verbs, form the simple past by adding *-ed* or *-d* to the plural present tense form, the one that doesn't end in *-s*. With irregular verbs, how the past tense is formed depends on the verb itself:

EXAMPLES: You **talked** about this very problem only a day ago.

Laura **chose** to work the extra shift.

The **simple future tense** shows what will take place in the future. Form the simple future tense for both regular and irregular verbs by adding *will* to the plural present form, the form that doesn't end in *-s:*

21

EXAMPLES: The officers **will talk** with every witness to the robbery.

Colby **will choose** the most effective company logo.

The Perfect Tenses

The perfect forms of a verb indicate that something has already been completed relative to some other action or event. Create the perfect tense of a verb by adding a form of *have* to the verb's past participle. With regular verbs, the past participle is the same as the past tense form, the simple form of the verb ending in *-ed* or *-d*. With irregular verbs, the form of the past participle depends on the verb itself.

The **present perfect tense** shows that something has occurred sometime in the past or that something begun in the past may still be ongoing. Form it by adding either *has* or *have* to the past participle:

EXAMPLES: The emergency room specialist **has talked** to the man with the head injury.

My sister **has chosen** to return to school after a five-year absence.

The **past perfect tense** shows what has already happened in the past *before* something else happened in the past. Form it by adding *had* to the past participle:

EXAMPLES: The conductor **had talked** over the production with the entire orchestra.

The quarterback **had chosen** the play without consulting the coach.

The **future perfect tense** shows that something will happen by some point in the future. Form the future perfect by adding *will have* to the past participle:

EXAMPLES: By Friday, the mayoral candidates **will have talked** to more than five thousand voters.

The committee **will have chosen** finalists for the position by the end of the week.

The Progressive Tenses

Each verb also has a set of progressive tenses. In this context, progressive indicates that something is going on or was or will be happening. To

21

show this progress, use the present participle—a verb form ending in -*ing*—along with a form of the verb *to be: am, is, was, will be,* and so on.

The **present progressive tense** shows that something is currently ongoing. Create it by adding a present tense form of *to be—am, is, are—* to the present participle:

EXAMPLES: Right now, Antoine **is talking** to the ticket agent.

You **are choosing** the best possible car for your financial situation.

The **past progressive tense** shows that something was ongoing in the past. Form it by adding *was* or *were* to the present participle:

EXAMPLES: The players **were talking** to the assistant coach.

The candidate **was choosing** her words carefully to be sure not to offend anybody.

The **future progressive tense** shows that something will be ongoing into the future. Form it by adding *will be* to the present participle:

EXAMPLES: People **will be talking** about this party for months.

The franchise **will be choosing** its official mascot next week.

The Perfect Progressive Tenses

The perfect progressive forms of a verb indicate that an action, event, or situation that began at one point has been continuing or will have been going on in relation to some other action, event, or situation. Create the perfect progressive tense by adding *has been, have been, had been,* or *will have been* to the present participle, the -*ing* form.

The **present perfect progressive tense** shows that something began in the past and is still ongoing. Form it by adding *has been* or *have been* to the present participle:

EXAMPLES: My aunt **has been talking** about her vacation for more than two hours.

The vice president **has been choosing** the location for the annual meeting for more than a decade.

The **past perfect progressive tense** talks about something that had been happening in the past but stopped before the present. Form the past perfect progressive tense by adding *had been* to the present participle:

EXAMPLES: The two attorneys **had been talking** about the accidents before the insurance adjuster arrived.

The health club staff **had been choosing** this month's weight-loss champ when the video crew from the local television station arrived.

The **future perfect progressive tense** shows that something will be ongoing in the future but will conclude before something else begins. Form the future perfect progressive tense by adding *will have been* to the progressive form:

EXAMPLES: Those ten dissenting senators **will have been talking** about the proposed law for close to 10 hours by the end of today's session.

In June, the Trustees of the Agnes Kidd Memorial Fund **will have been choosing** scholarship recipients for 50 years.

The Modal Auxiliary Verbs

You can adjust or alter the meaning of a verb by adding some form of one of the **modal auxiliaries**—*can, shall, may, will,* and so on—to it. Consider how the addition of a modal auxiliary changes the meanings of *talk:*

EXAMPLES: She **could have been talking** to the police, but she refused out of fear.

Louie **would have talked** about his winning hit, but he was too modest.

The director of the health department **should be talking** more about the dangers of infectious diseases.

The clerk **may have been talking** on the phone when the fire started.

In the first sentence, *could have been* indicates what might have happened but didn't, and in the second, *would have* indicates what

21

was supposed to happen but didn't. In the third, *should be* indicates something desired that isn't happening, and in the fourth, *may have been* indicates a possibility that something occurred.

Maintaining Consistency in Verb Tense

As you present your ideas, be sure to be consistent in the verb tense you use. For a discussion about a previous event, it makes sense to use a form of the past tense. For a discussion about some attitude or issue at this moment, it makes sense to use a form of the present tense, and for a discussion about plans to be completed, it makes sense to use a form of the future tense.

What you need to avoid is a sudden switch from one tense to another:

Faulty: When Sheryl **walked** *[past]* into the club, her friends inside **jumped** *[past]* up. The next thing she **knows,** *[present]* the hostess at the counter **places** *[present]* a crown on her head and **begins** *[present]* to sing "Happy Birthday." As Sheryl **joined** *[past]* her friends, they **laugh** *[present]* loudly and **started** *[past]* to take pictures.

Here, half of the story is told in the past tense—**walked, jumped, joined, started**—and half is told in the present tense—**knows, places, begins, laugh.** The result is confusion for the reader.

To help ensure that your ideas come across clearly, make all the verbs either present tense:

EXAMPLE: When Sheryl **walks** into the club, her friends inside **jump** up. The next thing she **knows,** the hostess at the counter **placed** a crown on her head and **begins** to sing "Happy Birthday." As she **joins** her friends, they **laugh** loudly and **start** to take pictures.

or past tense:

EXAMPLE: When Sheryl **walked** into the club, her friends inside **jumped** up. The next thing she **knew,** the hostess at the counter **placed** a crown on her head and **began** to sing "Happy Birthday." As she **joined** her friends, they **laughed** loudly and **started** to take pictures.

Employing the Proper Verb Voice

21

With verb use, an additional consideration is **voice**—how a verb expresses the action or discussion relative to its subject. In the **active voice,** the subject does, has done, or will do the action, so employing the active voice accentuates this sense of action. A verb is in the **passive voice** when the subject is being acted upon: The *phone was answered.* You present a verb in the passive voice by adding a form of the verb *to be*—*is, were, could have been, might be,* and so on—to the past participle.

Consider these two sets of sentences, each set showing passive and active voice verbs:

>   *subject*   *verb*
> **Active:**   The *top American runner* **set** a new record in the 800-meter run.

>   *subject*   *verb*
> **Passive:** A new *record* in the 800-meter run **was set** by the top American runner.

>   *subject*   *verb*
> **Active:**   The *hospital* **scheduled** the procedure for 10 a.m.

>   *subject*   *verb*
> **Passive:** The *procedure* **has been scheduled** for 10 a.m. by the hospital.

As you can see, the active voice makes a sentence more direct. The subjects *perform* the action: *the top American runner* **set** the record and *the hospital* **scheduled** the procedure. An added advantage is that because sentences with active voice verbs generally contain fewer words, they are also more concise—brief but to the point.

With the verb in the passive voice, the subjects are *acted upon.* The reader has to wait until the end of the sentence to discover who actually set the record or scheduled the procedure. Thus the message is less direct and longer—with no improvement in detail or clarity.

However, you may on occasion find the use of the passive voice appropriate. Consider these pairs of sentences:

>   *subject*   *verb*
> **Passive:** During the party, *the new lamp* in the living room **was broken.**

>   *subject* *verb*
> **Active:** During the party, *someone* **broke** the new lamp in the living room.

21

subject   *verb*

Passive: *A $10,000 diamond watch* **was worn** by the model.

subject   *verb*

Active: *The model* **wore** a $10,000 watch.

With the first pair of sentences, the passive voice version is a good choice because whoever broke the lamp is unknown. And with the second pair of sentences, the passive voice version is more appropriate because the extraordinary value of the watch has more impact than the anonymous model wearing it.

    With verb voice, keep in mind that you are not making a choice based on correctness but on clarity. Active voice verbs are more direct and concise and thus better serve the needs of your reader. Therefore, make the active voice your default choice and stick with it unless you can make a case that the passive voice is more suitable in a particular sentence.

22

Noun and Pronoun Use

Using Naming Words Correctly

To keep the world straight, we name everything around us. The names assigned to people, places, things, and ideas are called nouns. The words often used in place of nouns are called pronouns, with *pro-* meaning "in place of." Pronouns function the same way in sentences that nouns do, and the use of pronouns helps to eliminate the needless repetition that would result if you simply used the same nouns over and over. To ensure that you use these types of words correctly, you need to focus on

- the function and forms of nouns
- the different cases of pronouns
- consistency in pronoun number
- clear relationships between pronouns and antecedents

You will find that you rely heavily on nouns and pronouns in the sentences you compose. Therefore, a solid understanding of how to use them properly will help keep your writing simple, clear, and correct.

22 The Function and Form of Nouns

Nouns are classified into two groups. **Common nouns** name non-specific people or things—an executive, a state, a novel. **Proper nouns** name particular people or things—Peter Kyd, Idaho, *The Bluest Eye*—and these nouns always begin with a capital letter. Nouns also have two forms, *singular* for those nouns referring to individual persons or things and *plural* for those nouns referring to more than one person or thing.

The Roles Nouns Perform

Of all the parts of speech in English, nouns are the most versatile, performing six distinct functions in a sentence:

- a **subject:**

EXAMPLE: **Yoga** has grown in popularity over the last decades.

- a **predicate nominative,** the word that answers "Who or What?" after a linking verb:

EXAMPLE: My cousin is a **detective.**

- a **direct object,** the word that answers "Whom or What?" after an action verb:

EXAMPLE: Unfortunately, the pilot left her **BlackBerry** in a restaurant.

- an **indirect object,** the word that answers "To Whom or For Whom?" or "To What or For What?" after an action verb:

EXAMPLE: After their argument, my sister sent her **boyfriend** an apologetic e-mail.

- an **object of a preposition,** the word that follows a preposition and completes a prepositional phrase:

EXAMPLE: The guitar in that **stand** once belonged to Eric Clapton.

- an **appositive,** a word that helps to explain or illustrate another noun:

EXAMPLE: They took their seats in the second row, the best **spot** to see action on stage.

Singular and Plural Forms

Regardless of a noun's function, you must always select the proper form—singular or plural—for each situation. To make most nouns plural, simply add -s to the singular form:

Singular	Plural
table	tables
book	books

Not all nouns form their plurals the same way, though. For example, to make most words that end in -*ch, -sh, -x,* or -*s* plural, add -*es:*

Singular	Plural
mix	mixes
brush	brushes
watch	watches
boss	bosses

For words that end in a consonant and -*y,* change the -*y* to -*i* and add -*es:*

Singular	Plural
candy	candies
mystery	mysteries

If words end in a vowel and -*y,* just add -*s:*

Singular	Plural
play	plays
key	keys

To make many words that end in -*f* or -*fe* plural, change the ending to -*ves:*

Singular	Plural
thief	thieves
wife	wives

However, some nouns ending in -*f* or -*fe* form their plurals by adding an -*s:*

Singular	Plural
chief	chiefs
safe	safes

22

To make combined or hyphenated words plural, add -s to the main word:

Singular	Plural
sister-in-law	sisters-in-law
passerby	passersby

To make some common words plural, you must change letters within the word:

Singular	Plural
child	child**ren**
louse	l**ice**
tooth	t**ee**th
woman	wom**en**

Some words have the same singular and plural forms:

Singular	Plural
species	species
deer	deer
fish	fish
sheep	sheep

Of course, these guidelines don't cover all nouns. For example, some words that end in -o, such as *trio* and *radio,* form their plural by adding -s. Other words that end in -o, such as *potato* and *echo,* form their plural by adding -es. Some words from foreign languages, such as *analysis* and *crisis,* form their plurals in keeping with their original language: *analyses* and *crises.*

When you are in doubt about the plural form of a noun, turn to the dictionary. It gives the plural ending in boldface for nouns that do not form a plural simply by adding -s.

Singular Nouns Ending in -s and Collective Nouns

Not all nouns that end in -s are plural. Singular nouns that end in -s include

economics	mathematics	mumps	physics	statistics
ethics	measles	news	politics	

Because these words end in *-s*, it's easy to incorrectly select a plural verb form, but they take singular verb forms:

EXAMPLE: In terms of areas of study, **ethics** *provides* an important foundation for many other academic areas.

Collective nouns are singular words representing groups of items or people. Common collective nouns include

audience	department	government	office
class	faculty	group	school
committee	family	herd	team
congregation	flock	jury	troop

Because they are intended to represent an entire group as a single unit, collective nouns call for a singular form of a verb:

EXAMPLES: Lindsey's **family** *owns* several small businesses.

Cue Words That Identify Number

When they appear immediately in front of a noun, *cue words* can help you decide whether a noun used as a subject needs a singular or a plural verb form.

The following cue words signal that a singular noun follows:

a, an	every
another	neither
each	one
either	

EXAMPLES: **Each** musician in the quartet *plays* a solo during the concert.

One sculpture *attracts* more visitors than any other item in the museum.

The following cue words generally signify that a plural noun follows:

all	many
both	several
few	some

22

EXAMPLES: **Several** deer *feed* in my backyard every evening.

Both drivers *receive* support from several major corporations.

The singular and plural cue words (except for *a* and *an*) may also serve as pronoun subjects. In this use, they are usually followed by a prepositional phrase beginning with *of.*

Singular   **One** of the comedians at the comedy club actually *works* as an accountant during the day.

Plural   **Few** of the rescued dolphins *seem* healthy enough to be released back into the ocean.

The Different Aspects of Pronouns

Pronouns take the place of nouns and do exactly what nouns do in a sentence. Mastery of pronouns involves recognizing a number of different aspects related to their use, including choosing proper pronoun case and maintaining clear agreement between a pronoun and a verb and between a pronoun and its antecedent.

Considering the Different Cases of Pronouns

Personal pronouns, which refer to specific persons, places, and things, change in form, or *case,* depending on their use:

PERSONAL PRONOUNS

	NOMINATIVE CASE		OBJECTIVE CASE		POSSESSIVE CASE	
	Singular	Plural	Singular	Plural	Singular	Plural
First Person	I	we	me	us	my/mine	our/ours
Second Person	you	you	you	you	your/yours	your/yours
Third Person	he, she, it	they	him, her, it	them	his, her/hers, its	their/theirs

As the table shows, each case has three divisions, first, second, and third person. Use first-person pronouns to talk about yourself, second-person pronouns to address someone directly, and third-person pronouns to discuss other people or things.

When a personal pronoun is the subject or predicate nominative, the **nominative case** is the correct choice:

plural nominative
EXAMPLE: **They** began cheering as soon as the team stepped onto
subject
the field.

singular nominative
EXAMPLE: The focus of the TV news report was **she.**
predicate nominative

When a personal pronoun is the object in a sentence—a direct object, an indirect object, or an object of a preposition—the **objective case** is the correct choice:

singular objective
EXAMPLE: Rosie called **them** about the party.
direct object

plural objective
EXAMPLE: The company gave its **customers** a big discount.
indirect object

singular objective
EXAMPLE: He kept the extra keys in the top **drawer.**
object of the preposition

When the personal pronoun shows ownership, the **possessive case** is the correct choice:

singular possessive
EXAMPLE: That blind date was the best night of **his** life.

plural possessive
EXAMPLE: Ultimately, **their** friends all agreed with the decision to cancel the neighborhood reunion.

The relative/interrogative pronoun *who* also has three forms:

Nominative Case	**Objective Case**	**Possessive Case**
who	*whom*	*whose*

subject
EXAMPLE: The person **who** encouraged me to return to school was my brother Joseph.

object of the preposition
EXAMPLE: The person to **whom** she is most grateful is her grandmother.

sign of ownership
EXAMPLE: One person **whose** confidence inspires me is my Uncle Carlos.

22

Personal Pronouns as a Part of Compound Subjects or Objects   One complication with personal pronoun use occurs when the pronoun is part of a compound subject or object. Consider the pairs of pronouns in parentheses in the following sentences:

EXAMPLES: Tyesha, Alana, Rayleene, and (I/me) always meet at the back of the cafeteria for lunch on Wednesdays.

Between you and (I/me), that band isn't very good.

To make the correct choice, identify what role the personal pronoun is serving in the sentence. In the first sentence, the pronoun is part of the compound subject, so the nominative form, *I*, is the correct choice. In the second sentence, the personal pronoun is part of the compound object of the preposition *Between*, so the objective form, *me*, is the correct choice.

Personal Pronouns in Elliptical Constructions   Another challenge with personal pronoun use involves elliptical constructions, shortened forms of sentences beginning with *than* or *as*. Elliptical passages aren't spelled out because the missing sections are understood. To figure out which personal pronoun to use, spell out the understood part of the sentence. Consider the pairs of pronouns in parentheses in the following sentences:

EXAMPLES: Valerie has a much better personality than (he/him).

The social workers are more concerned about James than (she/her).

With the first sentence, the complete meaning is, "Valerie has a better personality than he has," so the correct choice is the nominative case, *he*.

The second sentence represents a more complex problem because the meaning changes depending on which case form you choose. Choose the nominative form and you are actually saying, "The social workers are more concerned about James than she is concerned about James." Choose the objective form and you are actually saying, "The social workers are more concerned about James than they are worried about her." Therefore with this type of elliptical construction, it's a good idea to finish the construction in your head or on paper and then write down the shortened form that represents your actual meaning.

Issues with Possessive Case Pronouns

Confusion between the possessive form of some personal pronouns and the contractions that sound like them represents another potential problem. One pair that is commonly confused is the possessive pronoun *its* and *it's*, the contraction for *it is* or *it has*. The possessive pronoun *its* is already possessive, so no apostrophe is needed.

To avoid making this error, check if *it is* or *it has* fits the sentence. If it does, you want *it's*. If not, use *its*. Consider the words in parentheses in the following two sentences:

EXAMPLES: (Its/It's) too early to purchase tickets for the playoff game.

The pit bull was barking loudly and trying to chew through (its/it's) leash.

The first sentence needs *It is* to communicate the meaning, so *It's* is the correct choice. But in the second, *it is* doesn't make sense, so *its* is the correct choice.

Other potentially troublesome pairs are *your/you're, their/they're,* and *whose/who's*. To ensure that you choose the correct word, see if the two words making up the contraction (*you are, they are, who is,* or *who has*) fit the sentence. If so, use the contraction. If not, choose the possessive form of the personal pronoun.

Incidentally, any time you use a pronoun before a gerund, the proper choice is the possessive case:

EXAMPLE: The board of the youth center appreciated his coaching the pee-wee basketball team.

Singulars and Plurals with Indefinite Pronouns

Some **indefinite pronouns**—words that represent nonspecific people, places, things, and ideas—are always singular:

another	everybody	nothing
anybody	everyone	one
anyone	everything	somebody
anything	neither	someone
each	no one	something
either	nobody	

22

Some of them are always plural:

both, few, many, several

And some of them are either singular or plural depending on the word they refer to, called the antecedent:

all, any, more, most, none, some

Several indefinite pronouns hold the potential for error, in particular the singular indefinite pronouns *everybody* and *everyone*. Because these words suggest or encompass many people, you may find yourself using them as if they were plural, as this example shows:

Faulty: **Everyone** needs to bring *their* workout clothes.

Everyone is singular, but the word it refers to—its antecedent—is plural, so the sentence contains an error in **pronoun–antecedent agreement.**

To correct this kind of error, simply make the two words match in number:

                    singular   *singular*
Corrected: **Everyone** needs to bring *his or her* workout clothes.

            or

                plural   *plural*
All participants need to bring *their* workout clothes.

In general, the better choice with sentences like these is to make both words plural because the plural version simply flows better.

You may encounter the same kind of difficulty with *anybody, anyone, nobody, no one, somebody,* and *someone*. When you use one of these words, make sure that the pronoun and its antecedent are both the same number.

A Clear Relationship between Pronoun and Antecedent

For your reader to understand your ideas, you must make sure that the relationship between each pronoun and its antecedent is clear. Look at this sentence:

Ambiguous: During the play, **Joe** and **John** smashed into each other, and **he** broke **his** nose.

22

The relationship between the pronouns and their antecedents is ambiguous, and this lack of clarity prevents the reader from understanding who did what to whom.

To eliminate this kind of ambiguity, restate the sentence completely:

Corrected: During the play, Joe and John smashed into each other, and **John** broke **Joe's** nose.

The pronoun *it* holds the same potential for confusion. Look at this example:

Ambiguous: Fontelle made a mess when she poured ice water from the pitcher into the glass because **it** was cracked.

The pronoun **it** has two potential antecedents, *pitcher* and *glass,* so you need to specify which of the two objects was cracked, as these two versions show:

Corrected: Fontelle made a mess when she poured ice water from the pitcher into the glass because **the pitcher** was cracked.

or

Fontelle made a mess when she poured ice water from the pitcher into the glass because **the glass** was cracked.

23

Adjective, Adverb, and Other Modifier Use

Using Modifying Words Properly

To make sure that what you write is clear, vivid, and strong for your reader, you need to make it specific, detailed, and precise. The words that enable you to meet this goal are called **modifiers,** language that describes or limits other words in a sentence. As Chapter 14, "Parts of Speech," spells out, **adjectives** modify nouns (and occasionally pronouns), and **adverbs** modify verbs, adjectives, and other adverbs. To ensure that you use modifiers correctly, you need to concentrate on a few key features, including

- different forms of adjectives and adverbs, including commonly confused and irregular modifiers
- intensifying and absolute modifiers
- dangling and misplaced modifiers

Adjectives and adverbs are among a writer's most powerful tools. Learning how to identify and eliminate errors in modifier use will go a long way to making your writing simple, clear, and correct.

Using the Correct Forms of Adjectives and Adverbs

Adjectives and adverbs have three separate forms: **positive, comparative,** and **superlative.** Regular modifiers follow predictable patterns as they change from one form to the next. The positive form of a regular modifier is the basic version of the word, for example, *young* or *reasonable.*

The comparative form casts one thing against another. For regular one-syllable modifiers, the comparative form consists of the positive form plus *-er: younger.* With regular modifiers of more than two syllables, the comparative form consists of *more* before the modifier: *more reasonable.*

The superlative form singles out one item from several as outstanding or extreme. With a regular modifier of one syllable, the superlative form consists of *-est* added to the positive form—*youngest.* With a regular modifier of more than two syllables, the superlative form consists of *most* before the modifier—*most reasonable.*

When it comes to regular modifiers of two syllables, no single rule governs the creation of the comparative and superlative forms. Some two-syllable modifiers, for instance, *happy,* consist of the positive form plus *-er* or *-est: happier, happiest.* Other two-syllable modifiers, *private,* for example, consist of *more* or *most* in front of the modifier: *more private, most private.* Therefore, unless you are absolutely sure of the proper form of two-syllable modifiers, always check a dictionary to find the correct form.

Remember this point as well: regardless of the number of syllables, never use both *more* and *-er* or both *most* and *-est* with the same modifier. Modifiers like *more slower* and *most carefulest* are always wrong.

Things are much simpler with negative comparisons. Except with irregular modifiers, negative comparisons are created the same way: *less* before the modifier with a comparison of two items, situations, individuals, etc., and *least* before the modifier with a comparison of three or more:

EXAMPLE: The controversial speaker seemed less **worried** than the head of security about safety. In fact, he appeared to be the *least* **concerned** person in the entire room.

23 Dealing with Commonly Confused and Irregular Modifiers

A number of modifiers are irregular, so you can't rely on the rules for forming the comparative and superlative forms of regular modifiers to guide you. Here is a list of common irregular modifiers:

Positive	Comparative	Superlative
bad	worse	worst
badly	worse	worst
good	better	best
little	less	least
much	more	most
well	better	best

Actually, deciding between *good* and *well* and between *bad* and *badly* probably causes the most headaches. *Good* and *bad* are adjectives. They describe people, objects, and ideas. *Well* and *badly* are adverbs. They describe how a person or thing performs an action. A person can be a good or bad dancer but <u>cannot</u> dance good or dance bad. When you talk about how someone does something, you need an adverb: She *sings <u>well</u>* but *dances <u>badly</u>*.

Note that *bad* and *badly* share the same comparative and superlative forms, as do *good* and *well*. *Bad* and *good* are adjectives, modifying nouns or pronouns. *Badly* and *well* are adverbs, modifying verbs, adjectives, or other adverbs. *Worse* and *worst* and *better* and *best* can be either adjectives or adverbs, depending on how you use them. Simply remember that *worse* and *better* are the comparative forms and that *worst* and *best* are the superlative forms of these irregular modifiers, and you will be all set:

Comparative: Of the two violinists at the audition, Greta *performed* **worse.**

Superlative: Of all the people I know, Clyde has the **worst** *temper*.

Comparative: The point guard for our team has a **better** *jump shot* than her opponent.

Superlative: The most recent Xbox features the **best** *graphics* of any gaming system.

Dealing with Intensifying and Absolute Modifiers

Two types of modifiers that require a little extra attention are **intensifying modifiers** and **absolute modifiers.** Intensifying modifiers are adverbs used to strengthen or emphasize other modifiers. Common intensifiers include *actually, definitely, much, really, so, too,* and *very.* The problem with these words is that, by themselves, they generally don't provide much added strength or emphasis to the words they modify, as these examples show:

EXAMPLES: The area near the beach was **very** *cold*.

The fans were **really** *excited* when the singer returned for an encore.

The difference between *cold* and *very cold* or *excited* and *really excited* isn't specific or vivid. Rather than using an intensifying modifier, look for a single word that pins down what you are trying to say. Instead of *very cold*, write *chilly* or *frigid* or *raw*, and instead of *really excited*, try *electrified* or *exhilarated* or *elated*.

Absolute modifiers represent an extreme, something that can't logically be compared to anything else, so they have no comparative or superlative forms. Such words also can't be accentuated in any way, so don't combine them with intensifying modifiers.

Take a word like *unique*, for instance. *Unique* means "one of a kind." To say that a video game is *very unique* doesn't make sense because uniqueness is a quality that can't be compared—nothing equals it. Something is either *perfect* or imperfect, *impossible* or possible, *round* or not round, *straight* or not straight. A person can't be <u>extremely</u> dead or <u>somewhat</u> equal or <u>especially</u> round. It's either one or the other. Thus, when you use an absolute modifier, be sure you let it stand on its own, without any intensifier.

Avoiding Dangling and Misplaced Modifiers

It's important to place modifiers in your sentences so that they help you communicate your ideas to your reader. In this regard, you need to be concerned about **dangling** and **misplaced modifiers.**

Recognizing and Correcting Dangling Modifiers

A dangling modifier is a word or group of words, usually appearing at the beginning of a sentence, that lacks an appropriate word

23

to modify. The sentence may suggest or imply what the dangling modifier is supposed to describe or illustrate, but the word itself is missing. Look, for instance, at these examples, with the dangling modifiers underlined:

Dangling: <u>While preparing dinner</u>, the doorbell rang.

Dangling: <u>To perform effectively</u>, regular practice is a necessity.

In this form, these sentences don't make sense. In the first example, the phrase *While preparing dinner* appears to modify *doorbell*. In the second, the phrase *To perform effectively* appears to modify *regular practice*. Certainly, a reader might be able to figure out what was intended, but your job as a writer is not to make your readers have to figure out what you mean.

To correct a dangling modifier, adjust the phrasing in the sentence so that the modifying phrase clearly describes or limits the appropriate word:

Corrected: While preparing dinner, **Maya heard** the doorbell ring.

or

While **Maya was** preparing dinner, the doorbell rang.

Corrected: To perform effectively, **you must practice regularly**.

or

Practicing regularly **will help you perform effectively**.

Recognizing and Correcting Misplaced Modifiers

When you write, you know the word you want a modifier to describe or illustrate, regardless of where it appears in the sentence. But your reader doesn't share your insight. Therefore, if the modifiers in your sentences are misplaced, that is, not near the words they modify, your reader won't get the full understanding of your message.

Consider these examples:

Misplaced: *As a toddler,* Ellen's grandfather often took Ellen to the park.

Misplaced: The sales representative demonstrated the light, compact tablet computer for the customer *with all the latest apps.*

Misplaced modifiers prevent sentences from making sense. *As a toddler* in the first example seems to modify *Ellen's grandfather*, and *with all the latest apps* in the second example seems to modify *customer*.

But a toddler can't be a grandfather. *As a toddler* is meant to modify *Ellen*. And humans don't come *with all the latest apps*. This phrase is obviously intended to modify *light, compact tablet computer*.

To correct these errors, place the modifiers next to the words they modify, or restate the sentence in some way so that it makes logical sense:

Corrected: **As a toddler,** Ellen often went to the park with her grandfather.

or

When she was a toddler, her grandfather often took Ellen to the park.

Corrected: The sales representative demonstrated the light, compact tablet computer **with all the latest apps** for the customer.

or

The customer asked the sales representative for a demonstration of the light, compact tablet computer **with all the latest apps.**

The use of qualifying modifiers, including *almost, even, just, nearly,* and *only,* can also be challenging. If you don't place these modifiers near the words they modify, they'll change the meaning of your sentence. Look at these examples:

EXAMPLES: My cousin **nearly** paid $200 for a counterfeit Rolex watch.

My cousin paid **nearly** $200 for a counterfeit Rolex watch.

In the first sentence, **nearly** modifies *paid*, indicating that the cousin was thinking about buying the counterfeit watch but for some reason didn't follow through. But in the second, **nearly** modifies *$200*, indicating that the cousin did buy the counterfeit watch but paid somewhat less than $200 for it.

23

Of the limiting modifiers, *only* is probably the most frequently used and misused. Look at these versions of the same sentence, with *only* in different positions:

EXAMPLE: **Only** Caitlyn was amused by what the instructor was saying today.

- Of all the students, Caitlyn alone was amused.

EXAMPLE: Caitlyn was **only** amused by what the instructor was saying today.

- Although other reactions were possible, Caitlyn's reaction was limited to being amused.

EXAMPLE: Caitlyn was amused **only** by what the instructor was saying today.

- Nothing on that day except the instructor's comments amused Caitlyn.

EXAMPLE: Caitlyn was amused by what the instructor was saying **only** today.

- The instructor's comments amused Caitlyn on this one day alone; normally she did not find the comments funny.

The point is that words like *only* alter the meanings of the words you use them to modify, and that's an advantage for you as a writer. Simply make sure to place them with the words you want them to modify. That way, the message that your reader receives will be the one you intended to send.

24

Spelling

OVERVIEW

Mastering the Rules and the Exceptions

If you have difficulty spelling, you can point to a number of good reasons for at least some of your errors. Although some English words conform to spelling rules, others don't necessarily follow consistent spelling patterns. Some words—*psychotic, though, gnat,* for example—are not spelled the way they sound. Other words, such as *to, too,* and *two,* sound the same but are spelled differently and have different meanings. In short, spelling seems hard because it often is. However, difficult or not, spelling *always* counts. Your reader always expects correct spelling, and errors in spelling are major distractions from your good ideas. Furthermore, spelling errors may lead some readers, especially those who find spelling easy, to discount the value of your thinking. The good news, however, is that several techniques can help you develop greater mastery of spelling, including

- a thorough review of basic spelling rules and exceptions to these rules
- a careful study of commonly confused words
- a close examination of frequently misspelled words

These techniques will enable you to develop a personal spelling dictionary that is tailored to your own particular spelling problems and will help you keep everything you write simple, clear, and correct.

24 ## Remembering the Basic Rules of Spelling

To strengthen your spelling skills, master the following rules governing the majority of English words. Pay particular attention to the exceptions to the rules, as these exceptions are often among the most frequently misspelled words.

Making Words Plural

Make most words plural by adding -s to the singular form. A number of words don't conform to this simple rule, including

Nouns that end in -ch, -sh, -x, and -s Form the plural of nouns that end in -ch, -sh, -x, and -s by adding -es:

birch birches	box boxes	lash lashes

Nouns that end in -y For most words ending in -y, use the letter preceding the final letter as a guide. If that letter is a vowel (a, e, i, o, u), simply add -s:

toy toys	key keys	tray trays

Exceptions Don't change proper names. *Murphy* becomes *Murphys*, not *Murphies*.

If the letter before the -y is a consonant, change the -y to -i and add -es:

story stories	duty duties	sky skies

Nouns that end in -o If the letter preceding the final -o is a vowel, simply add -s:

radio radios	stereo stereos	trio trios

If the letter before the -o is a consonant, add -es:

potato potatoes	echo echoes	veto vetoes

Exceptions Some nouns related to music, such as *altos, falsettos, solos,* and *sopranos,* do not follow this rule. In addition, a few nouns ending in -o preceded by a consonant can end in either -s or -es:

cargo cargos *or* cargoes	motto mottos *or* mottoes
zero zeros *or* zeroes	

Words that end in -f or -fe Add an -s to form the plural of some nouns that end in -f or -fe:

safe safes	belief beliefs	chief chiefs

For others, change the *-f* to *-ves:*

half hal**ves**   knife kni**ves**   leaf lea**ves**

For some nouns ending in *-f* or *-fe,* two forms are acceptable:

scarf scarfs *or* scar**ves**   hoof hoofs *or* hoo**ves**
dwarf dwarfs *or* dwar**ves**

When in doubt, always check the dictionary.

Nouns with Latin endings   In general, form the plurals of nouns with Latin endings in keeping with the original language:

alumnus alumn**i**   crisis cris**es**   analysis analys**es**

With other words from Latin, add *-s* or *-es* to form the plural:

appendix   appendix**es** *or* appendi**ces**

memorandum   memorand**a** *or* memorand**ums**

index   ind**exes** *or* indi**ces**

Hyphenated and combined nouns   Form the plural of hyphenated and combined nouns by adding *-s* to the main word:

sister**s**-in-law   leftover**s**   attorney**s** general

Irregular plurals   Form the plural of several common words by changing letters within the word or by adding letters to the end:

woman wom**en**   tooth te**eth**   child child**ren**

Nouns with the same singular and plural forms   Remember that a handful of common words have the same form whether they are singular or plural:

one deer   several deer   one sheep   many sheep
one species   five species

Nonword plurals and words discussed as words   Form the plurals of abbreviations, figures, numbers, letters, words discussed as words, and acronyms by adding either *-s* or *-'s* (apostrophe + *-s*). Use *-'s* with all lowercase letters, with the capital letters *A, I,* and *U,* or any other time when adding *-s* alone might confuse the reader:

one *A*   four *A's*   one *i*   several *i's*   one *the*   many *the's*

24

Dealing with Prefixes and Suffixes

A **prefix** is a unit such as *un-, dis-, mis-,* or *semi-* added to the beginning of a word. When you add a prefix to a word, do not change the spelling of the word:

believable **un**believable   agree **dis**agree   conscious **semi**conscious

A **suffix** is a unit such as *-ness, -ing,* or *-ous* added to the end of a word. Whether the spelling of the basic word changes depends on the suffix being added.

- For the most part, don't change the spelling of the original word when adding *-ly* or *-ness:*

    usual usual**ly**   faithful faithful**ness**   rare rare**ly**

    But for words with more than one syllable that end in *-y,* change the *-y* to *-i* before you add *-ly* or *-ness:*

    lonely lonel**iness**   easy eas**ily**   silly sill**iness**

    Exception   When you add *-ly* to *true,* you drop the final *-e: truly.*

- For words ending in *-e,* drop the final *-e* when adding a suffix beginning with a vowel:

    cope cop**ing**   disapprove disapprov**al**   fame fam**ous**

- Keep the final *-e* if the suffix begins with a consonant:

    care care**ful**   arrange arrange**ment**   safe safe**ty**

    Exceptions   Drop the final *-e* in the following words with suffixes beginning with a consonant:

    whole who**lly**   argue argu**ment**   judge judg**ment**

    But keep the final *-e* in these words:

    mileage   peaceable   noticeable   courageous

- For words ending in *-y* preceded by a consonant, change the *-y* to *-i* before you add a suffix, unless the suffix itself begins with *-i:*

    bury bur**ied**   simplify simpl**ified**

                    but

    hurry hurr**ying**   identify identif**ying**

- Double the final consonant for one-syllable words that end in a single consonant preceded by a single vowel before adding a suffix beginning with a vowel:

plan plan**ned**   slip slip**ping**   flat flat**ten**

However, if the final consonant is preceded by another consonant or by more than one vowel, just add the suffix beginning with a vowel:

wash wash**ed**   warn warn**ing**   fail fail**ure**

With a word of more than one syllable ending in a single consonant preceded by a single vowel, you need to say the word out loud to identify where the emphasis or accent belongs. If the accent is on the final syllable, double the final consonant before adding the suffix:

begin begin**ning**   admit admit**ted**   occur occur**rence**

But if the accent is not on the final syllable, simply add the suffix:

benefit benefi**ted**   profit profit**able**   abandon abandon**ing**

Working with Words with *ie* or *ei* Combinations

Here is a simple rhyme generations of U.S. schoolchildren have learned that encapsulates the basic rule for words with *ie* or *ei* combinations:

I before *e*
Except after *c*
And when sounded like *a*
As in *neighbor* or *weigh*

The two vowels in the following words create a long *e* sound and do not follow *c*, so the correct combination is *ie:*

grief   believe   field   achieve   hygiene

The two vowels in these words **do** follow *c*, so the correct combination is *ei:*

receive   perceive   ceiling   conceive   deceive

And the two vowels in these words have an *a* sound, so the correct combination is also *ei:*

beige   freight   eight   vein   heinous

24

Exceptions The letter *e* comes before *i* in the words *either, neither, leisure, seize, their,* and *weird* even though the combination doesn't follow *c* or sound like *a*. And in *species, science, prescient, society,* and *ancient, i* comes before *e* even though the letters **do** follow *c*.

Understanding Basic Rules for *-sede, -ceed,* and *-cede* and Other Endings That Sound Alike

Spelling a word in English based solely on how it sounds is generally not a good strategy. Sometimes, a syllable or sound within a word has more than one spelling, and sometimes one word sounds like another that is grammatically incorrect for the situation.

Words that end in *-sede, -ceed,* and *-cede* Only one word in English ends in *-sede:*

supersede

Only three words in English end in *-ceed:*

proceed   exceed   succeed

All other words with this sound end in *-cede:*

precede   secede   intercede

Have **versus** *of* The correct forms *could've, should've,* and *would've* sound like the incorrect forms *could of, should of,* and *would of.* Therefore, never trust your ear. Always write the full correct form—*could have, should have,* and *would have*—first. If for some reason you find the contraction form more appropriate, make the change in the final draft.

Used to **and** *supposed to* In most cases, it is nearly impossible to hear the final *-d* in the expressions *used to* and *supposed to.* As a result, these two expressions are frequently misspelled as *use to* and *suppose to,* and computerized spelling- and grammar-checking software often doesn't recognize the errors. Therefore, always add the final *-d* in *used* and *supposed,* even if you don't hear the sound of the letter.

A lot **and** *all right* These two common expression are frequently misspelled as *alot* and *alright.* Always use the standard, two-word versions, *a lot* and *all right.*

Dealing with Commonly Confused Words

24

Some spelling errors aren't actually a result of misspelling but rather of incorrectly chosen words. Often the words in question are sound-alike words like **homonyms** (sometimes called **homophones**), which sound like the correct words but have different spellings and meanings. To eliminate errors of this kind, carefully review the following list of commonly confused words, along with their definitions and sentences containing the words used properly. Concentrate in particular on words that have previously given you difficulty.

accept—take or receive
except—leave out, excluding, but

EXAMPLES: The man displaced by the fire declined to **accept** any assistance.

Except for a sweatshirt supplied by the police department, he even refused donations to replace his lost clothing.

advice—opinions, suggestions
advise—give suggestions, guide

EXAMPLES: My high school guidance counselor usually gave me sound **advice**.

But when I asked her to **advise** me about college, she didn't do a good job.

affect—influence, stir the emotions
effect—a result, something brought about by a cause

EXAMPLES: The weather in the spring always **affects** her health.

The first **effect** I notice is that she begins wheezing.

all ready—everyone or everything prepared
already—before, previously

EXAMPLES: By noon, we were **all ready** to begin the annual beach clean-up.

The city had **already** delivered two trash dumpsters for us to fill.

24

among—within more than two
between—within two

EXAMPLES: At the reunion, Michelle sat **among** several classmates.

She took a seat **between** her two best friends from high school.

brake—device to stop; come to a halt
break—shatter; pause

EXAMPLES: As soon as the ambulance shot into the intersection, I stomped on the **brake.**

For a moment, I was sure that the pedal would **break** off.

can—be physically able to
may—have permission to

EXAMPLES: Even young children **can** learn to play a musical instrument.

Some of them **may** develop a lifelong interest in performing.

choose—decide or select (present tense)
chose—decided or selected (past tense)

EXAMPLES: With a little luck, the owners will **choose** a better coach this time.

Week after week, the former coach simply **chose** the wrong game plan.

conscience—inner sense of right and wrong
conscious—aware, awake

EXAMPLES: The senator said that his **conscience** led him to admit his involvement in the bribery scandal.

Conscious of the possibility of a recall election, he hoped to appear contrite to the voters.

council—a group formally working together
counsel—give advice; legal representative

EXAMPLES: The town **council** discussed the proposed reductions in their operating budget.

The town solicitor tried to **counsel** the members to consider that the only other alternative was to increase property taxes.

desert—abandon; dry, arid, sandy place
dessert—final part of a meal

EXAMPLES: The old concrete soccer stadium was as hot and dry as a **desert**.

After the first half hour, people at the picnic began to **desert** the area, heading to a nearby air-conditioned ice-cream parlor for a cool **dessert**.

fewer—refers to items that can be counted
less—refers to amounts or quantities that can't be counted

EXAMPLES: The Midwest had **fewer** tornados last year.

In addition, this region experienced **less** flooding.

good—used to describe persons, places, things, and ideas
well—used to specify how something is, was, or would be done

EXAMPLES: After only a few weeks of class, Curtis has become a **good** painter.

No one should be surprised because he could always draw **well**.

hear—listen
here—refers to specific direction or location

EXAMPLES: With all the noise in the subway station, it was nearly impossible to **hear** the list of canceled trains.

At least **here** in this station, all announcements also appear on a screen above the entrance.

hole—an empty spot
whole—complete

EXAMPLES: The explosion blew a large **hole** in the roof of the abandoned house.

As a safety measure, officials evacuated the **whole** neighborhood.

24

its—possessive form of *it*
it's—contraction for *it is* and *it has*

EXAMPLES: As the crew hoisted the piano up to the second floor, they acted slowly to ensure that the heavy instrument didn't shift in **its** harness.

It's always the most dangerous step involved in this kind of move.

knew—understand, past tense
new—recent, not old

EXAMPLES: When I saw people lined up outside the electronics store, I **knew** exactly what was going on.

A **new** version of *Overtime*, a popular computer game, was finally for sale.

know—understand
no—negative, the opposite of *yes*
now—at this point

EXAMPLES: You certainly **know** my main complaint.

On most nights, the workers at the front end of the store get **no** help from the rest of the staff.

My concern is what the manager is going to do **now** to make sure that everyone is treated fairly.

lay—place down, spread out
lie—rest or recline

EXAMPLES: First, **lay** the mat on an area of the floor where you'll have room to move your arms and legs freely.

Then **lie** down on the mat and begin the first stretching exercise the chair.

lead—go first, direct, present tense (rhymes with *bead*); soft metal, graphite (rhymes with *bed*)
led—go first, direct, past tense

EXAMPLES: At the sound of the starter's pistol, Billy sprinted into the **lead**.

After the first 200 yards, he felt like he had **lead** weights on his ankles.

Before he reached the finish line, everyone he had initially **led** passed him.

24

loose—not tight
lose—misplace, fail, not win

EXAMPLES: As the car passed us, we saw that one of the wheels was wobbling, as if it were **loose**.

A minute later, the whole axle broke off, which caused the driver to **lose** control of the car and crash into the guard rail.

of—stemming from, connected with or to
off—away from, no longer on

EXAMPLES: As Peter and Penny left the apartment complex last night, Penny tripped on the edge **of** the sidewalk.

The problem was that someone had shut **off** the lights at the building's entrance, making it difficult to see.

passed—go beyond or by, past tense
past—time gone by, former time

EXAMPLES: The two men walked toward each other, glared, and then **passed** without saying a word.

Something had obviously happened in their **past** that was still not resolved.

personal—individual, private
personnel—employees, office or official in charge of hiring

EXAMPLES: On the job, your marital status is a **personal** matter.

The **personnel** office needs to be informed, however, for tax and insurance purposes.

precede—come before
proceed—go on

EXAMPLES: A brief announcement about the location of fire exits always **precedes** a performance in that auditorium.

Following the show, the audience **proceeds** through those exits into the cool night air.

24

principal—individual in charge; primary
principle—rule, law

EXAMPLES: My high school **principal** was especially strict about unauthorized cell-phone use during class time.

Her **principal** intent was to keep students focused on their schoolwork.

She reinforced the **principle** every day, sometimes confiscating as many as 20 phones in a single morning.

quiet—not noisy; solitude
quite—very, really

EXAMPLES: At the end of the trail, the woods were perfectly **quiet**.

The atmosphere was **quite** different from the scene at the head of the trail near the highway.

than—used in comparisons
then—next, at that time

EXAMPLES: When it comes to testing, I actually prefer to take an essay exam **than** to complete multiple choice or true and false assessments.

I read each essay question slowly and carefully and **then** restate it as the first sentence of my answer.

their—the possessive form of *they*
there—refers to a specific direction or location
they're—contraction for *they are*

EXAMPLES: The proponents of the offshore wind farm did a good job making **their** case to the state regulators.

For more than a year, **there** have been a series of hearings about the impact of the proposed wind farm on migrating birds and spawning fish. Thus far, the regulators say **they're** still not sure what the evidence actually shows.

24

though—despite, however
thought—idea, process of reasoning
tough—difficult, rough, hardy

EXAMPLES: At first glance, the fly ball seemed to land in fair territory, **though** it was hard to gauge from where I was sitting.

When the runner crossed the plate, we all **thought** that the game was over.

After a few moments, the home plate umpire waved the ball foul, a **tough** break for the Sox.

threw—toss, hurl, past tense of *throw*
through—in one side and out the other, from beginning to end

EXAMPLES: The two older men **threw** their horseshoes with great accuracy.

As the horseshoes flew **through** the air, they rotated a couple of times and hit the post with a loud *clang*.

to—in the direction of, toward (also used to form an infinitive)
too—also, excessively
two—more than one, less than three

EXAMPLES: The little boy handed the envelope **to** the teacher.

He was **too** shy and embarrassed to speak as he handed her a small package, **too**.

He then returned to his seat, glad to have delivered the **two** items.

waist—middle part of the body
waste—use up needlessly; leftover material

EXAMPLES: Before entering the tiny crawl space, the utility worker wrapped a rope around his **waist**.

Inside, he found several sealed containers labeled "Industrial **Waste**."

weak—not strong, feeble
week—seven days

EXAMPLES: After the volleyball game, Maria felt **weak**.

She probably shouldn't have played because she had not been feeling well for a **week** or so.

24

weather—atmospheric conditions
whether—indicating alternatives or options

EXAMPLES: Before we make our final plans for the day, we need to check the long-range forecast to see what the **weather** will be like.

Still, the committee has decided to go ahead with the celebration **whether** the forecast indicates rain or sunshine.

were—past tense of *are*
we're—contraction for *we are* or *we were*
where—indicates or raises a question about a specific direction or location
wear—have on

EXAMPLES: Although Lonnie, Spence, and I **were** planning on going to the gym, I was called into work, so **we're** going this week, instead.

We'll meet near school **where** there is free parking, and **wear** our sweats, so we won't even have to carry our gym bags.

who—nominative or subjective form, used as a subject
whom—objective form, used as an object

EXAMPLES: The tutoring center identified a student **who** could use my assistance with his biology class.

From the information the tutoring center provided, I felt that he was someone **whom** I could actually help.

who's—contraction for *who is* and *who has*
whose—possessive form for *who*

EXAMPLES: **Who's** in charge of cleaning the common area in the dorm this week?

No matter how hard I try, I can never seem to remember **whose** turn it is.

your—possessive form of *you*
you're—contraction for *you are*

EXAMPLES: **Your** new computer has the fastest processor available.

You're especially going to notice its speed when you have to download large files.

Mastering the Words That You Most Frequently Misspell

The following list contains words that people frequently misspell. To make this list work for you, you need to tailor it to your own needs. Read through the list with a pen, pencil, or highlighter in hand and mark the words that you have actually misspelled at some time or that are spelled differently than you thought. This shortened version will become the basis for your own *personal spelling dictionary*.

A computer file is the best place to maintain your personal spelling dictionary because it allows you to make adjustments as often as you need to. First, enter—double-spaced and in alphabetical order—the words you have identified from the list of commonly misspelled words as problems for you. Then insert any other words that have given you trouble in the past, including homonyms and other words discussed earlier in this chapter. Print the list out and keep it where you do your writing as a quick reference.

On a regular basis, update and reprint the list, adding words that you have misspelled in any of your academic papers and in your day-to-day writing. Make it a point to review the list at least once a week, focusing on the correct spelling of the words you use most often. If you follow these simple steps, you will be well on your way to becoming a better speller.

FREQUENTLY MISSPELLED WORDS

absence	acre	amateur	appreciate
academic	across	among	approach
acceptance	actual	amount	approval
accident	actually	analysis	argument
accidentally	address	analyze	arrival
accommodate	administration	angel	article
accompany	advertise	angle	ascended
accomplish	again	angry	assented
accumulate	agreeable	anonymous	association
accurate	aisle	answer	athlete
accustom	a lot	antarctic	attacked
ache	all right	anxious	attempt
achieve	although	apologize	attendance
acquaintance	aluminum	apparatus	attorney
acquired	always	apparent	authority

(continued)

24

FREQUENTLY MISSPELLED WORDS *(continued)*

auxiliary	certain	dealt	emphasize
available	change	debt	employee
awful	characteristic	deceased	envelop
awkward	cheap	decision	envelope
	chief	defense	environment
bachelor	children	definitely	equip
balance	church	definition	equipment
bargain	cigarette	dependent	equipped
basically	circuit	describe	especially
bath	cocoa	description	essential
bathe	collect	despair	exaggerated
beautiful	colonel	despise	excellent
because	color	diameter	excessive
beginning	colossal	diary	excitable
belief	column	different	exhausted
believe	comedy	direction	existence
benefit	comfortable	disappointment	experience
biscuits	commitment	disastrous	extraordinary
bookkeeping	committed	discipline	extremely
bottom	committee	discuss	
boundaries	company	disease	fallacy
breath	comparative	disgust	familiar
breathe	competent	distance	fascinate
brilliant	competitive	distinction	fatigue
Britain	conceivable	distinguish	February
bureau	condition	dominant	feminine
bury	consistent	dominate	fictitious
business	continuous	doubt	fiery
	convenience	dozen	foreign
cafeteria	cooperate	drowned	forty
calendar	cooperation	duplicate	fourth
campaign	corporation		freight
cannot	correspondence	earliest	frequent
careful	courteous	efficiency	fulfill
careless	courtesy	efficient	further
catastrophe	criticize	eligible	futile
category	curriculum	embarrass	
ceiling		embarrassment	garden
cemetery	daily	emergency	gauge
cereal	daughter	emphasis	general

generally
genuine
ghost
government
gracious
grammar
grateful
guarantee
guardian
guess
guest
guidance
gymnasium

handicapped
handkerchief
height
hoping
humor
humorous
hygiene
hypocrisy
hypocrite

illiterate
imaginative
immediately
immigrant
important
incidentally
incredible
independent
indictment
inevitable
infinite
inquiry
instead
intelligence
interest

interfere
interpret
irresistible
irreverent
island
isle

jealousy
jewelry
judgment

kitchen
knowledge
knuckles

language
later
latter
laugh
leave
legitimate
leisure
length
lengthen
lesson
letter
liable
library
license
lieutenant
lightning
literature
livelihood
lounge
luxury

machinery
maintain
maintenance

marriage
marry
marvelous
mathematics
measure
mechanical
medicine
medieval
merchandise
miniature
minimum
minute
miscellaneous
mischief
mischievous
missile
misspell
mistake
moderate
month
morning
mortgage
mountain
muscle
mustache
mutual
mysterious

naturally
necessary
necessity
negotiate
nickel
niece
noticeable
nuisance

obedience
obstacle

occasion
occurred
occurrence
official
often
omit
opinion
opponent
opportunity
oppose
optimism
organization
original
ought

pamphlet
parallel
paralyze
parentheses
participant
particularly
pastime
patience
peasant
peculiar
perceive
percentage
perform
performance
permanent
permitted
perseverance
personality
perspiration
persuade
phase
phenomenon
physical
physician

(continued)

24

FREQUENTLY MISSPELLED WORDS *(continued)*

picnic	receive	solemn	traitor
piece	recipient	sophisticated	transfer
pleasant	recognize	sophomore	transferring
politics	recommendation	souvenir	travel
possess	reference	specimen	traveled
possibility	referring	statistics	treasure
practically	regretting	statue	tremendous
precisely	reign	stature	truly
preferred	relevant	statute	Tuesday
prejudice	relieve	stomach	typical
preparation	remember	straight	
presence	remembrance	strategy	unanimous
pressure	reminisce	strength	urgent
primitive	removal	stretch	useful
priority	renewal	subsidize	utensil
privilege	repeat	substantial	
probably	repetition	substitute	vacancy
procedure	requirement	subtle	vacuum
professor	reservoir	sufficient	vain
protein	residence	summarize	valuable
psychology	resistance	superior	vane
publicity	responsibility	surprise	vegetable
pursuing	restaurant	surprising	vein
pursuit	rhythm	susceptible	vicinity
	ridiculous	suspicion	villain
qualified			violence
quality	salary	technique	visibility
quantity	sandwich	temperament	visitor
quarter	scenery	temperature	
question	schedule	tendency	warrant
questionnaire	scissors	theory	Wednesday
	secretary	thorough	writing
readily	sensible	thoroughly	written
realize	separate	tomorrow	
really	sergeant	tongue	yesterday
reasonably	severely	tournament	
receipt	similar	tragedy	zealous

25

Parallelism

Keeping It All Balanced

When you write, you frequently need to discuss similar or related ideas in the same sentence. In these cases, you must make sure that the ideas are expressed in matching or **parallel** form. Think of a playground seesaw. For the seesaw to function properly—for it to be balanced—what is on each side must be essentially the same. When you write, you create balance by presenting pairs—and groups—of connected words or phrases in a similar form. Incorrect parallelism distracts your reader, focusing attention on what doesn't match rather than on your good ideas. Therefore, understanding correct parallelism is a vital step in keeping your writing simple, clear, and correct.

25

With Individual Items

With a set of individual items, present all items in the same grammatical form. The coordinating conjunctions (*and, but, or,* and so on) are probably the most common means of connecting pairs or series of items. To make sure a series is parallel:

1. *Connect only similar parts of speech:* nouns with nouns, verbs with verbs, adjectives with adjectives, and so forth.

   EXAMPLE: Michael's voice is whiny, shrill, **and** ~~had a squeak~~.

   squeaky (above "had a squeak")

2. *Connect individual words in a series to other individual words but **not** to phrases or clauses.*

   EXAMPLE: M. Night Shyamalan is an *actor,* a *director,* **and**
   a screenwriter
   ~~he writes screenplays~~.

With a Series of Phrases

A phrase, as Chapter 15 explains, is a group of words without a subject and verb that acts as a single word. Common types of phrases include prepositional phrases and verbal phrases (-*ing* phrases and *to* + *verb* phrases). You can connect prepositional phrases with other prepositional phrases or *to* + *verb* phrases with other *to* + *verb* phrases. However, it is incorrect to connect prepositional phrases with verbal phrases or phrases with individual words, so simply change the incorrect element to a phrase that matches the others:

EXAMPLE: The accident affected drivers *at the scene, near the*
on the alternate routes
entrance ramps, **and** ~~the alternate routes were involved~~.

EXAMPLE: Jess enjoys physical activities, so every day you can find
running
her either biking, dancing, swimming, **or** ~~to run~~.

EXAMPLE: When you arrive at the station, be sure to call me **or**

to send a text message
~~texting~~.

CHAPTER 25 Parallelism **211**

With Items Connected by Correlative Conjunctions

As Chapter 14 notes, correlative conjunctions are pairs of connectors that indicate two possibilities, alternatives, conditions, and so on. Here again is a list of these conjunctions:

both/and	neither/nor	whether/or
either/or	not only/but also	

To eliminate faulty parallelism involving correlative conjunctions, make the second item match the first:

EXAMPLE: The new play was **not only** enjoyable
relevant
but also ~~its relevance was unmistakable~~.

EXAMPLE: The computer technician was **neither** *courteous* **nor**
competent
~~did she do competent work~~.

With Comparisons Connected by *than* or *as*

To correct faulty parallelism with comparisons connected by *than* or *as,* change the second unit so that it is expressed in the same way as the first:

EXAMPLE: In some areas of the country, NASCAR events are as
NFL games
popular **as** ~~to watch NFL games~~.

EXAMPLE: Many people would prefer to walk across hot coals
to give
than ~~giving~~ a speech.

26

Punctuation

Maintaining the Nuts and Bolts

Tune into any conversation, and you'll hear words, phrases, and ideas of all kinds pour out of the mouths of the speakers. As you listen, you'll hear starts and stops and changes in tone and pitch. These pauses and adjustments enable you as the listener to follow the points the speakers are making. When you write, words alone cannot provide these necessary signals. You need the set of symbols known as **punctuation** to guide your reader through your ideas. Punctuation falls into three main categories:

- **end punctuation**—periods, question marks, and exclamation points
- **pausing punctuation**—commas, semicolons, and colons
- **enclosing punctuation**—parentheses, dashes, and quotation marks

In addition, the apostrophe indicates ownership and helps to create contractions.

To keep your writing simple, clear, and correct, you need to learn the specialized functions of each type of punctuation.

End Punctuation

To indicate the stop at the end of a thought, you use one of the three marks of end punctuation: the period, the question mark, or the exclamation point.

The Period   Use a period to signal the end of a sentence that expresses a statement:

EXAMPLE: The dog howled at the sound of the fireworks in the distance.

Other Uses of the Period   Place a period

- between the dollars and cents in monetary amounts—$72.50
- before any decimal—98.6, .625
- as the elements of an **ellipsis,** a series of three spaced periods—...— that signifies that part of a direct quotation that does not change the original's meaning has been left out
- after most initials and abbreviations—W. G. Costa, Ph.D.; etc.; Jr.; a.m.

Exceptions   Don't use periods with

- U.S. Postal Service abbreviations for the names of the states—IA (Iowa), NE (Nebraska), DC (District of Columbia)
- the names of organizations that have chosen not to use periods— ABC, NOAA, UCONN

The Question Mark   Use a question mark at the end of a sentence that expresses a direct inquiry or query of some kind:

Direct Question: When did you last speak to Kenny?

But with a suggested or *indirect* question, use a period, *not* a question mark:

Indirect Question: I was wondering when you last spoke to Kenny.

The Exclamation Point   Use an exclamation point at the end of a sentence that expresses excitement or some other strong emotion:

EXAMPLE: Don't touch that wire!

26

Keep your use of exclamation points to a minimum. When an episode is thrilling or frightening, your words, rather than exclamation points, should communicate that sensation.

Pausing Punctuation

In writing, you signify natural pauses in speech by using one of three marks of punctuation: the comma, the semicolon, or the colon.

The Comma   Use commas in five primary situations:

- to indicate a pause between clauses connected by coordinating conjunctions (*and, or, but,* and so on), correlative conjunctions (*either/or, not only/but also, whether/or,* and so on), and subordinating conjunctions (*because, although, until,* and so on). The conjunction joins the clauses, but you also need to include a comma to provide the pause that accompanies the connection:

coordinating conjunction plus a comma

EXAMPLES: Those sunglasses look expensive, **but** they are reasonably priced.

correlative conjunctions plus a comma

Not only was the sales representative polite, **but** she was **also** efficient.

subordinating conjunction plus a comma

Although Gary and Courtney attended the same high school, they never met until last summer.

You don't usually need a comma after the subordinating conjunction if the clause it introduces doesn't appear first in the sentence, as these examples show:

EXAMPLES: Most of the dairy products in the store spoiled **before** the power was restored.

The air began to smell of sulfur **after** the wind shifted.

- to separate the items in a series connected by *and* or *or:*

EXAMPLE: Twice a month, Jacqueline drives two hours across the state, meets with her flute instructor, and then works on a number of techniques.

- to set off words, phrases, and ideas that interrupt the flow of the sentence:

EXAMPLE: With the built-in cameras on today's laptops, *however,* people can enjoy video chatting.

or that are *nonrestrictive,* meaning that they could be left out of the sentence without changing its full and accurate meaning:

nonrestrictive element

EXAMPLE: Yellowstone National Park, *which is among the world's most spectacular locations,* is actually part of a supervolcano.

If the material can't be left out without changing the sentence's meaning, though, the material is *restrictive,* and you don't enclose it in commas:

restrictive element

EXAMPLE: All cars **that have special stickers** may be parked on the grassy area next to the stadium.

Also, don't set off the names of close family members with commas:

EXAMPLE: **My brother** Edward is majoring in geology.

- to indicate a brief break between introductory material and the sentence itself:

If the introductory material consists of four or more words or contains a verb form, put a comma after it:

EXAMPLE: **After reading the e-mail,** my aunt suddenly began to cry.

Even if an introductory unit has fewer than four words, set it off from the rest of the sentence with a comma if the unit helps to emphasize the main idea of the sentence or makes the meaning of the sentence clearer for your reader. Clarifying expressions such as *of course, for example,* and *for instance* and common conjunctive adverbs such as *also, finally, however,* and *instead* fall into this category:

EXAMPLE: **Of course,** the patient's diet of junk food and excessive amounts of alcohol contributed to his poor physical condition.

- to set off a direct quotation from the rest of the sentence:

You signify a person's exact words—called a *direct quotation*—by enclosing them in quotation marks. With direct quotation, insert a comma to separate the speaker's words from the **attribution,** the phrasing that identifies the speaker. As the following examples show, you can place the quotation in three places within a sentence. In each case, use a comma to separate the direct quotation from the attribution.

26

EXAMPLES: "My phone isn't in my backpack," Nicole said quietly.

Nicole said quietly, "My phone isn't in my backpack."

"My phone," Nicole said quietly, "isn't in my backpack."

Use commas for a handful of other purposes, including:

- to set off the salutation of a personal letter—Dear Lauren,
- to separate elements in a date—March 31, 1982, was her birthday.
- to divide parts of an address—Mr. Kevin Sbardella, 325 Middle Street, Midville, GA 30441
- to signify hundreds within numbers of more than four digits, except decimals—1,254 or 5,400,768
- to set off a name in a direct address—But, Marcy, I don't agree with any part of your argument.

The Semicolon   As Chapter 19 explains, a semicolon is equivalent to a comma plus a conjunction—, **and**—but at the same time, a semicolon signals that the relationship between the units is so strong or so significant that no word is needed to link them.

EXAMPLE: Once the party was over, all she wanted to do was go to bed; the sound of a fire alarm down the hall changed her plans.

Adding a conjunctive adverb like *besides, finally,* or *therefore,* followed by a comma, after the semicolon can emphasize the relationship between the units:

EXAMPLE: Once the party was over, all she wanted to do was go to bed; **however,** the sound of a fire alarm down the hall changed her plans.

Use semicolons rather than commas to separate series of items such as names, dates, addresses, and so on, that contain commas themselves:

EXAMPLE: The scholarship recipients include Lukas Joseph, 12A Harrold Avenue, Swansea, NH; Nicholas Anderson, 12 Hardy Way, Banjo, WV; and Kathryn Spencer, 165 Wood Street, Corona, AZ.

The Colon   Use a colon to announce that something important—for example, an explanation, a list, a formal quotation of more than one sentence, and so on—is to follow:

26

EXAMPLE: The mayor then made the announcement for which the crowd was waiting: The City-View Drive-in Theater would be allowed to remain in business for another year.

Use colons in a few other instances, including:

- after the salutation of a formal letter—Dear Dr. Arakelian:
- between hours and minutes—10:45
- between the city of publication and the publishing company in bibliographic citations and footnotes—New York: Pearson Education
- between biblical chapter and verse—Genesis 4:11

Enclosing Punctuation

When you need to keep some ideas in your writing separate from the rest of the information, use one of the marks of enclosing punctuation: parentheses, dashes, or quotation marks.

Parentheses   Use parentheses to enclose information that not every reader necessarily needs—for instance, a definition, an explanation, or an expression of personal feelings:

EXAMPLES: In the back of the deli (the one on Main Street, not the one on Plymouth Avenue), the city health inspector found a serious problem.

Jaundice (yellowing of the skin and whites of the eyes) is a symptom of serious liver problems.

Include a mark of terminal punctuation if the unit within the parentheses is a complete sentence:

EXAMPLE: The price tag for the new bridge was a staggering $200 million. (When work on the bridge began a decade ago, the cost was estimated to be $120 million.)

26

The Dash   To make sure that an idea stands out, set it off with a dash (two unspaced hyphens):

EXAMPLES: At the conclusion of the date—and it was by far the worst date I had ever been on—he actually asked me out again.

But Becky had an advantage—acting experience—so she had a flawless interview.

Quotation Marks   Enclose a person's exact words within quotation marks.

Place a comma at the end of a direct quotation that opens a sentence to separate it from the attribution—the phrase indicating the speaker—and the rest of the sentence. If the quotation expresses strong surprise or a question, use an exclamation point or a question mark instead of this closing comma. Then put the appropriate mark of end punctuation after the rest of the sentence:

EXAMPLES: "I still can't believe that the town charges a $25 admission fee," said Jasmine.

"I still can't believe that the town charges a $25 admission fee!" said Jasmine.

If the direct quotation appears at the end of the sentence, place a comma before the opening quotation mark. The mark of end punctuation in the direct quotation serves the entire sentence, so you keep it within the closing quotation mark.

EXAMPLES: Jasmine said, "I still can't believe that the town charges a $25 admission fee."

Jasmine exclaimed, "I still can't believe that the town charges a $25 admission fee!"

And if part of the direct quotation appears at the beginning of the sentence and part of it at the end, treat the opening portion the way you would treat an entire quoted passage at the beginning of a sentence, and treat the second portion the way you would treat an entire quoted passage at the end of a sentence.

26

EXAMPLES: "I still can't believe," said Jasmine, "that the town charges a $25 admission fee."

"I still can't believe," exclaimed Jasmine, "that the town charges a $25 admission fee!"

Incidentally, begin a new paragraph each time you change speakers in **dialogue,** a passage that records the exact words of two or more speakers.

Include no quotation marks when you write an indirect quotation, which merely explains or states what a person said:

Direct   *exact words spoken*
Quotation: The confused driver said, "I never saw the stop sign."

Indirect   *report of the words spoken*
Quotation: The confused driver said that she never saw the stop sign.

Also use quotation marks to discuss the definition, origin, or specialized use or meaning of a word—She wanted to "unfriend" him as quickly as possible—and to enclose the titles of shorter works that can be thought of as parts of something larger:

Article title—"The Gulf Oil Spill's Unseen Damage"
Chapter title—"Concussions: The Broad Implications"
Short story title—"The Difficult Conversation"
Song title—"Smooth"
Episode of a TV show—"Secret Santa"

But put in italics the titles of the longer works from which they come:

Magazine name—*National Geographic*
Book title—*The Body Human*
Short story collection—*Crawdad: Tales from the Edge of Yesterday*
CD title—*Supernatural*
TV show—*The Office*

The Apostrophe

The **apostrophe** serves two primary functions: to show ownership in nouns and to form contractions.

26

To Show Possession   Making words possessive is simple:

- To change a singular noun into a possessive noun, add an apostrophe and -*s:*

EXAMPLES: musician's instrument   boy's jacket

zebra's stripes

Add an apostrophe and an -*s* even for singular words that already end in -*s:*

EXAMPLES: James's answer   boss's parking space

witness's concerns

If the resulting possessive form is awkward, replace it with a prepositional phrase. Rather than writing *James's answer,* write *the answer from James.*

- To make most plural nouns possessive, simply add an apostrophe:

EXAMPLES: musicians' instruments   boys' jackets

zebras' stripes

Make plural words that don't end in -*s* possessive by adding an apostrophe and -*s* to the plural noun:

EXAMPLES: men's shoes   people's backgrounds

children's games

- To make indefinite pronouns (*anybody, everybody, anyone, everyone, nobody,* and so on) possessive, add an apostrophe and an -*s:*

EXAMPLES: everybody's lunch   anyone's fault

nobody's intent

- If compound subjects jointly possess something, put an apostrophe and an -*s* after the last subject:

EXAMPLE: Maddy and David's truck [*one item jointly owned*]

If each subject possesses his or her own item, add an apostrophe and an -*s* to each subject:

EXAMPLE: Maddy's and David's paychecks [*two items separately owned*]

26

- To form the possessive of compound words like *maid of honor* and *father-in*-law and of business and corporation names that are compound, add an apostrophe and an *-s* to the end of the word:

EXAMPLES: sister-in-law's hobby
Attorney General's announcement
Ben & Jerry's ice cream

To Form Contractions   In a contraction, an apostrophe takes the place of the letters left out when the words are combined, as the following sentences show:

EXAMPLES: That tie definitely doesn't go with this shirt. (does + *not*)

If I had a choice, I'd rather be home reading a book.
(*I* + *would*)

Here is a list of common contractions:

COMMON CONTRACTIONS

aren't—are not	he's—he is, he has	should've—should have
can't—cannot	I'd—I would	that's—that is
couldn't—could not	I'll—I will	they'll—they will
didn't—did not	I'm—I am	they're—they are
doesn't—does not	isn't—is not	who's—who is, who has
don't—do not	it'll—it will	won't—will not
hadn't—had not	it's—it is, it has	you'd—you would
hasn't—has not	she'd—she would	you'll—you will
haven't—have not	she'll—she will	you're—you are
he'd—he would	she's—she is, she has	
he'll—he will	shouldn't—should not	

Notice that the letters in contractions follow the same order as in the original two words. The exception is *won't*, the contraction for *will not*.

A number of contractions are among the most frequently confused words, including

it's—its
they're—their—there
who's—whose
you're—your

26

To make sure that you choose the proper homonym, change the contraction back to the original two words—for example, *you're* back to *you are* or *it's* back to *it is* or *it has*—and read the sentence aloud. You'll be able to tell right away whether the contraction is correct.

Apostrophes serve a few additional functions, including:

- to replace numbers omitted from dates—the '60s (1960s)
- to mark time that is expressed in word form—five o'clock
- to create informal contractions—ID'd, OK'd
- to form the plurals of the capital letters *A, I,* and *U—A's, I's,* and *U's*
- to form the plurals of lowercase letters—*i's, b's,* and *e's*

27

Capitalization and Numbers

Specifying and Quantifying

Attention to detail is important in all aspects of your life, including writing. As you write, you need to be aware of and attend to certain details that will guide your reader through your ideas. These structural elements include

- *capitalization*—the system that involves the use of uppercase letters to stress the significance of some words
- *numbering*—the appropriate presentation of numerals in word or figure format

Proper capitalization and use of numbers emphasize to your reader that you are detail oriented. More important, correct use of these structural elements demonstrates your commitment to making everything you write simple, clear, and correct. That's what your reader always expects and always deserves.

27 Capitalization

Capitalization refers to the technique of making particular words stand out through the use of an uppercase or capital letter at the words' beginning. One strategy that will help you master capitalization is to focus on when words should be capitalized and when they shouldn't.

When to Capitalize

According to the basic rules of standard English usage, always capitalize

- the first word in a sentence:

EXAMPLE: The stairs leading down to the pool are especially slippery.

- the proper names of people, things, and places, including specific holidays, countries, states, cities, bodies of water, parks, historical periods or events, months, days of the week, planets, races, deities, religions, and nationalities:

EXAMPLES:
Krista Hays	Hispanic	Gulf War
Reformation	Croatian	Krishna
Glacier National Park	Venus	Lake Superior
Labor Day	Christianity	Nile
Antarctica	Asian	San Antonio

- the months and days of the week:

EXAMPLE: Yearly inspection reports must be completed by the second Monday in July.

- the personal pronoun *I:*

EXAMPLE: Moesha and I are hoping to go someplace warm during spring break.

- a word that designates a family relationship when you use that word as a part of, or as a substitute for, a specific name:

EXAMPLE: Sorrel and Greg always make time to visit Gramma and Aunt Vida.

- formal titles such as *reverend, senator, mayor,* and so on, when you use them in conjunction with a person's name:

EXAMPLE: Dr. Wong specializes in literature of John Steinbeck.

- words such as *street, avenue,* and *boulevard* when they are part of a specific address:

EXAMPLES: 49 Richmond Street   5A Washington Court

1700 Whipple Lane

- words such as *North* and *West* when they designate specific sections of a country:

EXAMPLE: Hundreds of miles of highway in the South and the Northeast are in deplorable condition.

- the names of languages and the main words of specific academic course titles:

EXAMPLE: Next semester, I plan to take Calculus II along with Spanish and American History 102.

- the first word and all main words in the titles of books, poems, newspapers, magazines, television shows, movies, and so on:

EXAMPLES: *The Naked and the Dead*   *Chicago Tribune*

Sports Illustrated   *There Will Be Blood*

"Fire and Ice"   *The Colbert Report*

- the names of specific brands, companies, clubs, and associations:

EXAMPLES: Oregon Road Runners Club   Under Armour

National Collegiate Athletic Association   Dell, Inc.

Kebbler   Eddie Bauer

- all letters of acronyms and abbreviations of proper names:

EXAMPLES: NEA (National Endowment for the Arts)

ABC (American Broadcasting Corporation)

NOAA (National Oceanic and Atmospheric Association)

27

- the first letters of the beginning of formal written correspondence, called the *salutation,* and the first word of the ending, called the *complimentary close:*

EXAMPLES: *Common Salutations*   *Common Complimentary Closings*

Dear Ms. Gutowski: **Respectfully,**

Dear Alex,   Sincerely,

- the first word in a direct quotation included in a sentence:

EXAMPLES: Before class began, Maria asked Brendan, "Did you remember to bring my notebook?"

"It's right here," Brendan replied.

- the first word of a complete sentence within parentheses:

EXAMPLE: The protesters outside the Statehouse were demanding that Representative Joan Jenard resign. (She had earlier sponsored a bill that would give a tax break to Central Gas and Power, which had just announced steep fee increases.)

- the first word of a line of poetry:

EXAMPLE: "Metaphors"

I'm a riddle in nine syllables,

An elephant, a ponderous house....

(Sylvia Plath)

Exception Modern verse doesn't always follow this guideline.

When *Not* to Capitalize

In addition to remembering when you should capitalize words, be sure that you

- *don't* capitalize the names of the seasons:

EXAMPLE: Last **spring,** we had cold and rainy weather right through the beginning of **summer.**

- *don't* capitalize the points on the compass when they indicate direction:

EXAMPLE: The nearest Coast Guard cutter is 20 miles south of the spot where the distress signal originated.

- *don't* capitalize the names of general school subjects:

EXAMPLE: With today's emphasis on state-wide assessments, many teachers worry that students are losing out on **art** and **music** education.

- *don't* capitalize words like *road, avenue, lane,* and so on, if they are not part of a specific address:

EXAMPLE: Those **streets** intersect with the oldest **avenue** in the city.

- *don't* capitalize the words *moon* or *earth* (unless *earth* is used as part of a list of planets):

EXAMPLE: When the **moon** comes closest to the **earth**, it's known as its *perigee*.

- *don't* capitalize titles or positions if they are not used as part of a name:

EXAMPLE: The **city councilors** need to meet with the **superintendent of schools**.

- *don't* capitalize *a, an,* or *the* or a preposition or conjunction of fewer than five letters when used as part of a title unless it is the first or last word:

EXAMPLES: *Pirates of the Caribbean*   *Less than a Treason*

   Of Mice and Men   "To an Athlete Dying Young"

The Correct Use of Numbers

Unless directed otherwise in the classroom or on the job, spell out numbers rather than use numerals when they

- begin a sentence and identify numbers of one or two words:

EXAMPLE: **Twenty-five** volunteers set up **two** disaster centers near the **five**-alarm blaze.

27

- express approximate amounts, age, time not identified as a.m. or p.m., fractional amounts used without a whole number, and street names under 100:

EXAMPLE: Around **nine** o'clock yesterday morning, **nearly twenty** dolphins, almost **three-quarters** of the pod, began beaching themselves at Shallows Beach, which abuts **Second** Avenue.

Use figures for numerical amounts that indicate

- precise measurements, decimals, fractions, monetary amounts including dollars and cents, highway numbers, and larger exact numbers:

EXAMPLES: **21** inches $^7/_8$ **6.2**   **$49.99**

Interstate **182**   **15,250**   **2,976,501**

- addresses, percentages, page numbers, book and play sections and divisions, times with a.m. and p.m designations, and days and years in dates:

EXAMPLES: **625** Cambridge Street   **54** percent   page **28**

Act **2**, Scene **1**,   Chapter **24**

10:48 a.m.   July **26, 1975**

Use a combination of words and figures to represent large amounts:

EXAMPLES: **200** million   **$8** billion   **4.5** trillion

With a passage containing related numbers, decide which form—word form or numeral form—is more appropriate for that context, and use that form consistently:

EXAMPLES: Contestant **101** had a much better voice than most of the other entrants, including contenders **4** and **14**, both finalists from the previous year.

The lawsuit threatened by **two** residents shouldn't carry more weight than a petition signed by **forty-three** of their neighbors.

With two unrelated numbers expressed in figure form next to each other, you have two options:

27

1. use a comma to separate the two numbers:

EXAMPLE: In **2011, 411** of the 1,345 sophomores in the district
           ranked as *superior* or *satisfactory* on the state's new
           American History Assessment.

2. or restate the sentence so that the numbers are no longer next
   to each other:

EXAMPLE: Of the 1,345 sophomores in the district who in **2011**
           took the state's new American History Assessment,
           411 ranked as *superior* or *satisfactory*.

Tips for Academic Success

Success in the classroom, like success in any aspect of life, is not an accident. Rather, it is the result of dedication, commitment, and hard work—and patience because success isn't always immediate or complete.

But make no mistake about it: you have more control over your destiny as a student than you might think. Don't hope for any magic formula. If success were that simple, it would be automatic. But the following guidelines will certainly put you on the path to academic success:

- **Take yourself and your work seriously, and make sure everyone else knows that you are committed to your studies.**
- **Consider the expression "You have only one chance to make a first impression."** The point is that you are responsible for your own image. If you want to show your classmates and your instructors that you are dedicated to your schoolwork, be sure to
  - **Show up on time for each class and stay for the entire class session.**
  - **Be prepared for class every time.** Have your books with you, your notebook open, your pen or pencil in hand ready to go—with extras just in case.
  - **Be completely in the room.** Don't let your focus wander. You paid for this experience. You wouldn't buy a ticket for a movie, concert, or sporting event and then not bother to

pay attention. School is more important to your future than those other events.

- **Be respectful of everyone in the room.** Don't interrupt or speak when classmates or the instructor is speaking. When you do talk, speak loudly enough so that everyone can hear you.
- **Use an appropriate tone of voice, even on those occasions when the discussion is heated or contentious.** The loudest person isn't necessarily the smartest, and neither is the person who tries to monopolize or dominate the discussion.

- **Get organized at home.** Learn the difference between being *proactive* and being *reactive*. For example, make sure you have the academic supplies you will need before you actually need them. The time to discover that you don't have the necessary paper or folder or that your printer is low on ink is not the night before an assignment is due. And don't wait until you are ready to walk out the door to gather what you need for school. Instead, arrange your backpack or book bag the night before.

- **Make your calendar your best friend.** At the beginning of the semester, each of your instructors distributes a syllabus, which contains a schedule for the course and includes due dates for tests, examinations, presentations, papers, and so on. Record this information on a calendar—either a hard-copy calendar or the one on your computer or phone—and then review and edit the listing regularly. That way, you will never be surprised to discover that an assignment or presentation is due.

- **Run the clock—don't let it run you.** Time management plays a huge role in your success. It is a truism that there are only so many hours in a day—or in a week or in a semester. From the first day of classes, you need to establish your study schedule for school. That means accounting for your time. The hours you are attending class, working at your job, fulfilling family obligations, commuting to school, and so on are important to note, in part because you will see exactly how busy you are. More important, however, this is time that is unavailable for you to do your schoolwork. With these hours blocked off, you'll more easily be able to mark down when you *will* study and complete your schoolwork every day.

- **Recognize the circumstances that allow you to do your best out-of-class work.** Think about it: Do you require absolute quiet? Do you prefer to work in a particular place, either at home or on campus? Do you work best early in the morning, in mid-afternoon, late at night? The sooner you figure this out, the better the quality of your work will be.

- **Be patient—not everyone learns at the same pace.** Your education isn't a sprint. It's a long-distance race, so give yourself a reasonable chance instead of walking away if you don't immediately develop the level of mastery that you had hoped for.

- **Pay no attention to the cliché that grades aren't important.** Of course grades are important, if for no other reason than to give you a sense of your overall progress. But no one grade is an absolute assessment of complete success or utter failure. Don't view a single grade as an enormous triumph or a terrible tragedy—it's just a measure at a particular moment.

- **On the first day of class, record in your notebook the office locations, phone extensions, and e-mail addresses of all your instructors.** That way, you'll always know exactly where this information is.

- **Make a connection with a classmate or two so that you can compare and share notes.** Doing so will also ensure that you have access to someone else's material should an emergency cause you to miss class.

- **Read actively.** Don't just let your eyes run across the words on a page. Instead, attack them. Approach all reading assignments with a highlighter or pen in hand. Think of active reading as a three-step process: *read, reason,* and *write.*

- **Regularly review your class notes.** Copy them over, and then prepare a summary. Writing about something is a great way to learn about it.

- **Turn your phone off as you walk into the classroom, put it away, and don't take it out again until you walk back out of the room.** You may not find it rude to check messages or send text messages during class, but others—especially your instructors—absolutely do.

- **Find and take advantage of every service—tutoring programs, study groups, writing centers, academic counseling, job placement centers, and so on—that your college offers.** Your tuition and fees support these services. In other words, you paid for them. Use them.

- **Don't ever, ever be afraid to be wrong in class.** Take a chance—answer that question. To give an incorrect answer isn't fatal. In fact, it may be the beginning of the best class discussion you have ever experienced.

Preparing a Summary

Writing an Effective Summary

As part of an assignment for some class or as a means of developing a greater understanding of a subject, you will often create a *summary*, a greatly condensed version of a document that still captures its essential message. In some fields, a summary is called an *abstract* or *précis*.

Depending on the length of the document itself, a summary may be as little as 5 to 10 percent the length of the original. In general, a summary should reduce the original by at least half, although the elimination of three-quarters is fairly typical.

An effective summary is the product of a series of steps. If you follow these steps, you'll find writing a summary much easier:

1. Read the original document *actively*.
   - Examine the title, introduction, headings and subheadings, conclusion, and other features designed to indicate the key points in the writing and make sure you understand their meanings.
   - Reread the writing, highlighting key ideas.

     Be on the lookout for **signal words** emphasizing importance, for example, *crucial, vital, significant, prominent,* or *extraordinary*. These words generally indicate the most important material.

     Study all charts, boxed information, or lists as well as specific names, dates, distances, amounts, conditions, and statistics. These elements often represent a brief version of what the writer considers important.

2. Make a list of the key ideas you've identified.
   - Express these ideas in your own words in complete sentence form.
   - Consult a dictionary for any word in the original document that is unfamiliar to you so that you express its meaning correctly.
3. Eliminate the *least* essential ideas from your preliminary list by
   - crossing out more than one reference to the same point;
   - trimming or discarding lengthy examples and explanations; and
   - cutting any material taken from footnotes.
4. Using the sentences you have written, create a first draft of your summary.
   - Include enough information so that the summary would make sense to someone who has not read the original.
   - Present the material in your summary in the same order as it appears in the original document.
   - Unless instructed otherwise, don't include your own opinion of the original.
   - Provide transition wherever it is needed so that your draft seems like a coherent paragraph and not just a list of sentences.
5. Revise your draft summary. Make sure
   - you have created a version that makes independent sense;
   - you have supplied sufficient transition;
   - you have eliminated any of your own commentary on the original; and
   - you have eliminated any errors in form.

Examining the Process of Preparing a Summary

Here's a brief passage from "Deep Dark Secrets," an article by Andrew Todhunter. This document, which appeared in the August 2010 edition of *National Geographic*, focuses on inland blue holes in the Bahamas—collapsed and flooded underwater caves hundreds of feet deep that scientists are just now beginning to explore and study.

Offshore flooded caves, so-called ocean blue holes, are extensions of the sea, subject to the same heavy tides and host to many of the same species found in the surrounding waters. Inland blue holes, however, are unlike any other environment on Earth, thanks largely to their geology and water chemistry. In these flooded caves, such as Stargate on Andros Island, the reduced tidal flow results in a sharp stratification of water chemistry. A thin lens of fresh water—supplied by rainfall—lies atop a denser layer of salt water. The freshwater lens acts as a lid, isolating the salt water from atmospheric oxygen and inhibiting bacteria from causing organic matter to decay. Bacteria in the zone just below the fresh water survive by exploiting sulfate (one of the salts in the water), generating hydrogen sulfide as a by-product. Known on land as swamp or sewer gas, hydrogen sulfide in higher doses can cause delirium and death.

As the steps in the process indicate, creating an effective summary begins with an identification of the most essential information and the elimination of less significant or unnecessary details and examples.

Here again is the passage, this time with the key ideas highlighted and the less important or unessential information crossed out:

Offshore flooded caves, so-called ocean blue holes, are extensions of the sea, subject to the same heavy tides and host to many of the same species found in the surrounding waters. Inland blue holes, however, are unlike any other environment on Earth, thanks largely to their geology and water chemistry. In these flooded caves, such as Stargate on Andros Island, the reduced tidal flow results in a sharp stratification of water chemistry. A thin lens of fresh water—supplied by rainfall—lies atop a denser layer of salt water. The freshwater lens acts as a lid, isolating the salt water from atmospheric oxygen and inhibiting bacteria from causing organic matter to decay. Bacteria in the zone just below the fresh water survive by exploiting sulfate (one of the salts in the water), generating hydrogen sulfide as a by-product. ~~Known on land as swamp or sewer gas, hydrogen sulfide~~ ~~in higher doses can cause delirium and death~~.

After the rest of the steps in the process have been followed, here is the summary that results:

Inland blue holes like Stargate on Andros Island are unlike any other environment on Earth. Water chemistry in these collapsed undersea caves changes because of reduced tidal flow. A surface layer of rainwater keeps oxygen from reaching the salt water below, restricting bacteria from eliminating organic matter in the water. Below this layer, other bacteria flourish, producing potentially toxic hydrogen sulfide.

The summary reduces the 156-word passage to 61 words—39 percent of the original—but it still captures and communicates the original's meaning. If you are preparing the summary for submission in one of your classes rather than just to help you master the material or prepare for an examination or assessment, remember to acknowledge the original document. Use the MLA format (shown below) or some other form of documentation that your instructor prefers.

Work Cited

Todhunter, Andrew. "Deep Dark Secrets." *National Geographic* Aug. 2010: 34–53. Print.

Index

Notes